MORE PRAISE FOR ELISSA WASHUTA'S
MY BODY IS A BOOK OF RULES

"BODIES ARE US. AND NOT. HOW DO WE FIGURE OUT WHICH IS WHICH? ELISSA WASHUTA TAKES YOU ON A FEARLESS RIDE OF SEX, DRUGS, MOOD DISORDERS, SELF-IMPROVEMENT, DIETING, INTERNET DATING, ETHNIC IDENTITY, AND WHY SHE ISN'T CATHOLIC ANYMORE. *MY BODY IS A BOOK OF RULES* IS A FUNNY, SCARY, UNPREDICTABLE BOOK; IT READS LIKE THE INSIDE OF YOUR OWN HEAD."

—SALLIE TISDALE
AUTHOR OF *TALK DIRTY TO ME*

"A GENRE-BENDING ODE TO THE BI-POLAR BRAIN, WASHUTA'S VENOMOUS, LYRICAL CHAPTERS LINK TO FORM A MEMOIR THAT'S DARING, VULNER-ABLE, CAUSTIC, AND RAW. READING THIS BOOK, YOU FIND YOURSELF IN A STARING CONTEST WITH A WRITER WHO WON'T LOOK AWAY—NOT FROM HER DEVASTATING BETRAYALS OF BODY AND BRAIN, NOR THE CHRONIC SEARCH FOR A CHEMICAL CURE. SHE EXPLORES THE NUANCES OF BLOOD QUANTUM, COSMO, CATECHISM, PSYCHOTHERAPY, PROMISCUITY, FENC-ING, AND *LAW & ORDER: SVU* IN A VOICE THAT EMBRACES ITS SELF-DEPRE-CATING, SELF-DESTRUCTIVE, HUMOROUS, BEDAZZLED CONTRADICTIONS."

—NICOLE HARDY
AUTHOR OF *CONFESSIONS OF A LATTER-DAY VIRGIN*

MY BODY IS A
BOOK OF RULES

ELISSA WASHUTA

Red Hen Press | *Pasadena, CA*

Cover design by Nicholas Smith
Layout design by Michelle Olaya-Marquez and Nicholas Smith

Library of Congress Cataloging-in-Publication Data
Washuta, Elissa.
 My body is a book of rules / Elissa Washuta. —First edition.
    pages cm
  ISBN 978-1-59709-969-1 (tradepaper : alk. paper)
   1. Washuta, Elissa. 2. Manic-depressive illness—Patients—United
States—Biography. 3. Indian women—North America—Biography. 4.
Indians of North America--Biography. 5. Indians of North America—
Ethnic identity. 6. College teachers—United States—Biography. I. Title.
  CT275.W316A3 2014
  970.004'97—dc23
                        2014007669

The National Endowment for the Arts, the Los Angeles County Arts
Commission, the Los Angeles Department of Cultural Affairs, the
Pasadena Arts & Culture Commission and the City of Pasadena
Cultural Affairs Division, and Sony Pictures Entertainment partially
support Red Hen Press.

  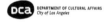

First Edition
Published by Red Hen Press
www.redhen.org

Acknowledgments

An earlier version of "Preliminary Bibliography" appeared in *Filter Literary Journal*.

An earlier version of "Prescribing Information" appeared in *Third Coast*.

Thank you to Artist Trust for their generous support of this book in the form of a GAP Award.

I am grateful to the many people who have lent me their time and expertise, along with the many others who have contributed to this book's development over the past several years.

To the wonderful people of Red Hen Press—thank you for all you have done for this book. Particular thanks go to Kate Gale and Nicelle Davis.

I am tremendously grateful to David Shields for the unceasing encouragement. To Maya Sonenberg, I am forever grateful for her challenges to me to create the best possible book.

The Cowlitz Indian Tribe has been an invaluable source of support—thank you for your commitment to my graduate education, and to my ongoing education as a human being.

To my colleagues in the Department of American Indian Studies at the University of Washington—thank you for your unwavering support of my writing.

Richard Hugo House has supported my development as a writer in more ways than I can name. Thank you to every person who has worked to build that beautiful place, and thank you to everyone who has come into my life because of it—you are so many, and I am so lucky.

My immense appreciation goes to Paullette Gaudet, Sarah Erickson, Chris Boginski, and Simone Sachs Hollander for being my first readers and for helping me build this book. Special thanks to Ann LoGerfo, Roz Ray, and Laura Scott for your insight in helping me wrench the near-final draft into place. Jon Sternfeld, thank you for your faith in this book and your eye for structural magic. Peter Mountford, I am greatly indebted to you for the wisdom you have imparted. Matt Hargis, thank you for providing records that were so important in writing this book, and for being there to keep them.

Brian McGuigan, huge thanks for opening up so many opportunities for me, for having my back, and of course, for being my friend.

Steve Barker, for your appraisal of every draft, for your unflinching encouragement at every turn, and for sticking around even after you heard me read the first chapter—thank you.

To my amazing family—here, there, and everywhere—aunts, uncles, cousins, Grandma, Grandpa, Mom, Dad, Nate—your love means everything to me. I am beyond grateful.

For Mom, Dad, and Nate

We are four chambers

Table of Contents

BODY MY HOUSE

MY HORSE MY HOUND

WHAT WILL I DO

WHEN YOU ARE FALLEN

   MAY SWENSON, "QUESTION"

THERE ARE WORSE THINGS THAN HAVING BEHAVED FOOLISHLY IN PUBLIC.

THERE ARE WORSE THINGS THAN THESE MINIATURE BETRAYALS,

COMMITTED OR ENDURED OR SUSPECTED; THERE ARE WORSE THINGS

THAN NOT BEING ABLE TO SLEEP FOR THINKING ABOUT THEM.

IT IS 5 A.M. ALL THE WORSE THINGS COME STALKING IN

AND STAND ICILY ABOUT THE BED LOOKING WORSE AND WORSE

AND WORSE.

   FLEUR ADCOCK, "THINGS"

MY BODY IS A BOOK OF RULES

A Cascade Autobiography

> *A girl who guarded her chastity was considered valuable in the eyes of our warriors. A man would willingly give many ponies and robes to her parents for such a wife.*
>
> MOURNING DOVE, *MOURNING DOVE: A SALISHAN AUTOBIOGRAPHY*

The Indians whom Sheridan had taken on the island were closely guarded. Old Chenoweth (chief) was brought up before Colonel Wright, tried, and sentenced to be hanged. The Cascade Indians, being under treaty, were adjudged guilty of treason in fighting. Chenoweth died game. He was hanged on the upper side of Mill creek. I acted as interpreter. He offered ten horses, two squaws and a little something to every "tyee" for his life, said he was afraid of the grave in the ground, and begged to be put into an Indian deadhouse. He gave a terrific warwhoop while the rope was being put around his neck. I thought he expected the Indians to come and rescue him. The rope did not work well; and, while hanging, he muttered, "Wake nica quas copa mamelouse!" He was then shot. The next day, Tecomeoc and Captain Jo were hanged. Captain Jo said all the Cascade Indians were in the fight. The next day, Tsy, Sim Lasselas and Four-fingered Johnny were hanged. The next day, Chenoweth Jim, Tumalth and Old Skein were hanged, and Kanewake sentenced, but reprieved on the scaffold. Nine in all were executed. Banaha is prisoner at Vancouver, and decorated with ball and chain. The rest of the Cascade Indians are on your island, and will be shot if seen off of it. Such are Colonel Wright's orders.

(From a letter by Lawrence W. Coe, describing the events of March 28, 1856, at the Cascades of the Columbia)

Tumalth begat Mary who begat Abbie who begat Kathleen who begat Leslie who begat Elissa.

The Dread

During my senior year of college, in the studio apartment the university paid for me to inhabit, as though I was more courtesan than scholarship show pony, I ignored all the helpful warnings handed down from the people in charge who did not seem to believe we children could keep ourselves alive. There were resident assistants roaming the floors, inspectors sniffing the apartments for smoke that had risen from some source other than charred pizza crust. There was the faceless university safety office that shot off missives into our mailboxes, card stock garishly printed to catch our attention but unable to compete with the issues of *Maxim* or *High Times* that we would pull from our mail cubbies, so any university notices would be dropped into the recycling, a homogenous stack. We deleted their e-mailed crime alerts and safety tips, too.

All the people who knew better than I did told me a thousand times to SNACK BEFORE AND DURING DRINKING, AVOID MIXING ALCOHOL WITH PRESCRIPTION MEDICATIONS. They said, PACE YOURSELF; they said, DO YOU KNOW HOW MANY DRINKS WITHIN A SHORT PERIOD OF TIME IS CONSIDERED BINGE DRINKING FOR FEMALES? If they wanted me to keep my ounces and hours straight, they shouldn't have asked me to measure my medicine numerically. I operated by my own logic: for my health, I drank Tropicana with immune-boosting Vitamin C that the carton promised me was dialed up to one hundred percent of what my body needed; for my pain, I added the crystal heat of Grey Goose, which I figured was sort of less unhealthy in its clarity. My liquid dinners delivered two servings of fruit, one serving of venom.

Beyond the walls of the brick compound I called home, there were the good people who worked on the third floor of the University Health Center: the woman who took my tearful appointment requests and refilled the displays of pamphlets on eating disorders, the therapist whose placement of the Zen rock garden on the table next to the patient's chair only made me suspicious, and the psychiatrist who supplied me with nearly as many mind-altering substances as the liquor warehouse outside the Beltway.

My windows opened to a busy street where student housing was stumbling distance from College Park's main bars. The strip mall across the street offered the four student food groups: burrito, noodles, rotisserie chicken, and coffee. Some bitter winters, grown children set couches aflame when Maryland lost to Duke, our archrivals who didn't feel the same way about us, their hate directed at UNC. The wave of rage seemed to strain against its impotence, desperate to make Duke know how much they were hated so that they would have no choice but to hate back. Riot cops rode through on horseback like Wild West sheriffs, plowing through drunks. In my hallway, the bulletin boards said, LOCK YOUR WINDOWS AND YOUR DOORS, but I slept under exposed screens, welcoming whatever danger might want to claw through the mesh to choke me out in the night. DO NOT PUT YOURSELF AT RISK, the health center's pamphlets told me. TALK TO SOMEONE YOU TRUST, they said. The girls' high heels would batter the sidewalk all night long. No matter the day of the week or the reading on the thermometer, a legion of ladies would pass by every few minutes, bound for the bars before midnight, the after-parties after. MAKE SURE SOMEONE KNOWS WHERE YOU ARE AT ALL TIMES. STICK WITH A "BUDDY." There wasn't only Grey Goose in my freezer: triple sec kept it company while six-packs of Red Stripe, Natty Boh, and Yuengling held down the fort in the fridge. That year, I slept less often than I passed out at the hands of liquor or prescribed pills, my whittled-down body nestled into the nook of my loveseat.

My closet bulged with defective dresses bought from the warehouse clothing store across the street that sold all the club wear the department stores couldn't move. The clothes were riddled with loose seams and the bold marks of G-Unit, Rocawear, Apple Bottoms, and other limp rejects from rappers' street wear lines. The only other clothing store in College Park was the one that sold bikinis.

On weeknights, I drew from my refrigerated reserves while I worked on the assignments that would continue to earn me the perfect "A" average I had maintained since I began to bring home report cards in my backpack from my Catholic grade school. I massacred the language sections of every standardized test. For the entirety of primary and secondary school, my only grade below an A was the seventh-grade B in gym class that my teacher paired with the report card comment, "Works to ability." School was my job, homework was my overtime, and my delayed payoff would be a hefty scholarship to the University of Maryland. First, I had to sit for an interview. I wondered, what was so special about me that the adults in suits around the interview table would want to hand me a sack filled with money? Not my poems about gorging myself on NyQuil and caffeine pills, not my miniature clay sculptures of the members of Nirvana, and not my gleaming transcripts—all the other students packing the waiting room put up equally brilliant numbers. When the smiling committee asked me to make myself special, I told them I was passionate about Indian issues. I was thousands of miles away from my nation of enrollment, the Cowlitz Tribe, but I had been reading a lot, and I said I wanted to use my education to work on problems in Indian country. I had just read this book that blew my mind and I told the nodding adults all about poverty and tradition and alcohol and loss.

I didn't know how to talk about the histories embedded in my bones, my great-grandmother's half-silence, the damming of our language that coincided with the damming of the Columbia River, my wordless conversations with the towering petroglyph woman and unmarked rocks by the water, my belly's swell that my mother told me was an Indian thing while I battled it with Weight Watchers point counts. I thought that if I told them all this, they would think all the Indianness had evaporated from my family line, leaving me pale and dry. So I told the adults, "I want to do something for my people," as I thought they wanted to hear, and two weeks later, I received a thin letter thick with the promise of more money than I could imagine: four years of tuition, room, board, and books.

Not long after installing my bell-bottom jeans and rainbow shower tote into my cinderblock closet freshman year, I told the kids on my floor of the honors dorm that in order to keep my scholarship, I'd have to obsess over every grade point. That money never went to white kids, I was told—it was practically a secret minority scholarship, so I must be an undercover genius. I'm not all white, I said. I'm Native American. "What's your SAT score?" they asked. "What was your GPA? What were your extracurriculars? How much Indian are you?" My parents taught me not to brag about matters of the brain. The first thing I learned in college was that white boys don't care if you're legitimately enrolled Cowlitz if they think you robbed their college education coffers of the hundred thousand dollars they worked toward through countless hours holding a tuba on a high school football field. They wanted me bundled as a sachet of sage, but they had no sense of the smell of it.

Next lesson: to make friends, drink. I didn't make friends for a long time.

By senior year, though, I was worked over into a new piece of woman. Even on weekends, I would sit at my desk, sipping on a screwdriver while cutting arguments out of my skull, until I would hear my friends shout to me through my open windows, telling me that they had come to rescue me: it was time to go out and get fucked up.

I would gulp down my drink, pull a dress out of my closet and shove it over myself before running out into the dark, starting below baseline lucidity, skipping in throwback Jordans toward the bars, certainly too far gone to consider that DRINKING IMPAIRS YOUR JUDGMENT, wanting nothing but more of it until the bars closed, at which point, if I wasn't busy trying to get anyone's number, I needed to make a run for the twenty-four-hour convenience store and clean out their supply of cheese-filled pretzels before the masses hit—that drunken indulgence, coupled with the mixed drinks, might be my only intake some days.

That year, while I worked toward leaving Maryland, my body, never a temple, became a haunted house. I tried to reduce the number of rooms I carried, shutting the doors on my love handles, narrowing the hallways of my loose upper arms, and collapsing the great hall of my gut. If I made myself into a tiny studio apartment, I reasoned, I might banish all the ghosts that clung to my bones. If only I had known that as the fat dissolved, the ghouls hiding in it would wake up and begin their rampage. I would get skinny, yes. Some days I would try so hard you'd think I was trying to burn this motherfucking house down.

I didn't care, though, that ALCOHOL CONTAINS CALORIES, and I cared even less that my pill bottles had told me every day for months DO NOT DRINK ALCOHOL WHILE YOU ARE USING THIS MEDICINE. Even though all three of the bars just off campus smelled like bleach and feet and offered little more than the chance to press into dark rooms full of unfamiliar bodies, we always lined up outside on weekend nights to get inside. During the summer, the bars were packed on weeknights, too, and we waited, hoping our pre-game intoxication wouldn't break while we stood. Rachel and Freda were my go-to girls for weeknight drinking, the perfect wingwomen, eternally up for pre-gaming, always effortlessly stunning, and always willing to lend a flask. Stick and I were poor wingmen for one another, because our opposite genders made us look like a couple, but we had a cross-gender bro-mance for the ages, completely platonic, so we would sometimes make separate laps around the bars before reuniting. Colin would appear from time to time, looking like an archival photo of an esteemed mid-century poet in his youth, trudging across blacktop in busted Top-Siders, sleeping-bagged in his worn khaki and flannel. He was enough of a partier that he had symptoms I couldn't attach to a particular poison, like regular morning blood loogies.

I came to know so well that VIRTUALLY EVERY ORGAN SYSTEM IS AFFECTED BY ALCOHOL. I made myself one rule for Cornerstone, Santa Fe, and Bentley's, our trifecta of destination drinking: no plastic cups of corrosive liquor from bottles beneath the bar. I stuck with beer or Stoli, or else my internal organs would dissolve into a coating in my mouth. YOU ARE THE ONLY PERSON WHO CAN KEEP YOURSELF SAFE, I knew.

From the moment I stepped into freshman orientation, I was told that COLLEGE LIVING CAN UNDOUBTEDLY BE EXCITING, but the truth, I came to learn, was that IT CAN ALSO BE A TIME OF UNSPEAKABLE TERROR, and though they told me so many times, DO NOT WALK ALONE AT NIGHT, in the middle of a meltdown, skittish and desperate to move, a 4 a.m. campus walk is safer than a drive, safer than hiding the knives, even if they're only put to use to make the little wake-up scratch that tempers the mood. NEVER HESITATE TO CALL UNIVERSITY POLICE, they said, but we all knew about what happened to kids who were honest with the people in charge about the severity of their problems: they were told to get the fuck out of college until they got their shit together. At least, that was what people said about my sensitive friend Henry, who collected perfume, top-shelf liquor, and cigars and wore his hair long so that he could keep curtains around his face. Supposedly, Henry was a suicide risk during his freshman year, and he was sent home for the remainder of it—too risky to keep him around. After I left, as he tried to wrap up his degree, he killed himself by combining alcohol and benzodiazepines, his final act of mixology, while alone in his on-campus apartment.

I never had any intentions to off myself—the doctors still ask me whether I ever did, and whether the thought crosses my mind now—but I did have to enlist the help of the campus mental health clinic during my last year of college, finding that too many mornings, I'd wake to find myself weighed down by dread and dolor. I would talk myself into getting out of bed by promising myself that, since I'd had an optimistic morning a few days before, one had to be coming soon, so I'd just have to work through this shitty day to reach it. I never missed work, rarely missed class. The only professors who knew about my stomach full of grubs were the ones to whom I bashfully passed doctor's notes requesting deadline extensions. My doctor simply wrote that I was under his care for treatment of major depressive disorder; he didn't tell them about my specific flavor of crazy, or that we were quickly working through drug changes to find one that would snap me into place.

I often wondered whether those people in charge really wanted to know the truth about our pain. I wondered whether their questions about how we were doing, what we were thinking, and whether we were holding up okay were just recitations. Those counselors and rulebook-wielding resident assistants said they wanted to help us, but we knew that all they wanted was to rinse their hands with their warnings. How could they help us if we told them the truth about the knots in our brainstems? I made my own way. I will tell you that the dread is long gone, a youthful buzz in my ears, something I worked through like a big girl, but know that it still hovers beyond the reaches of my eyeglasses and dusts every shot glass in my cupboard, waiting for me to relax.

A Cascade Autobiography

PART 2

I look white. You might think that means I am white. You are wrong. I have a photo ID card that says OFFICIAL TRIBAL above my official Indian grin—you know it's a legit tribal ID because the photographer didn't tell me to wipe the smile off my face. I suffer from gallbladder disease, of which Indians are at particular risk. I look vaguely Indian when I wear maroon and grow my hair long. Why can't the one-drop rule apply to me? I don't have just a drop of Indian blood—half my skull is Indian, or my two hands, one neck made of the same doomed substance as Tumalth's.

Note

University Health Center
University of Maryland
College Park, MD 20742

July 24, 2007

Campus Psychiatrists
Hall Health Center
Mental Health Clinic
University of Washington
Seattle, WA 98195-4410

To Whom It May Concern:

The patient requested her medical records as proof of her diagnosis and treatment as she prepares to move from Maryland to Seattle. We agreed that some of the contents of her medical records, especially notes on her mental state recorded by myself and her therapists, may be troubling to the patient. Therefore, I agreed to write this letter, which she can carry with her wherever she travels. These recollections have been gathered from my records and memories following our final appointment. Please use the following information as you wish.

The patient was first seen at the University of Maryland Mental Health Clinic in August of 2006 for symptoms of severe depression and anxiety. After completing a mood inventory upon her first visit, the patient scored 36 on the Beck Depression Inventory, indicating severe depression. We prescribed Lexapro.

The patient had consulted with a campus counselor in the spring of 2006 to deal with issues stemming from a sexual assault in January of 2005 ("Acquaintance rape"). The patient maintained a relationship with the young man despite his abusiveness. The patient exhibited no symptoms suggestive of PTSD. The patient discontinued counseling sessions due to concerns that her counselor failed to take her problems seriously (his primary suggestion for avoiding late-night meltdowns was to create an hour-by-hour schedule for evening activities [which, I agreed, was a flawed suggestion]).

We assigned her to one of our clinic therapists who, despite her training, cried when the patient detailed her wrung-out existence. The patient felt that the therapist's miniature Zen rock garden stationed next to the patient's chair, complete with sand and a tiny rake with which to move it around, was insulting to her emotional intelligence. The patient excelled in her English classes and maintained a 4.0 GPA.

The patient visited my office almost weekly while we worked to stabilize her moods. The patient was a regular fixture at the clinic. She saw me for drug adjustments more often than most patients see talk therapists. Although the patient's knowledge of psychopharmaceuticals could have caused concern that she may have been "medication-seeking," I instead saw this as a remarkable desire to understand her own drug regimen and possible future treatments. The patient was med-compliant to a nearly unmatched degree, exhibiting a complete willingness to improve her mental state through drug treatment. I disclosed to the patient that she was my favorite patient. Upon hearing this, the patient nodded and reported that she was only ever sane in doctors' offices.

The patient exhibited no developmental problems. The patient had no family history of psychiatric disorders. The patient grew up in a loving family. The patient had many friends on campus. The patient reported no prior history of alcohol or substance abuse, but, on occasion, she came to my office straight from class, stinking of booze. When I asked her about it, she replied that she had come from her creative writing workshop, and I had to admit that some of the greats were drunks.

The patient's mood gradually improved over the weeks following the use of Lexapro; however, following a setback, we added Wellbutrin for mood, low motivation, and daytime sedation. In addition, we added PRN Ativan for episodic anxiety.

The patient described nightly treks across campus to sit in a tunnel. The patient also described walks toward dangerous neighborhoods, cut short by fatigue. The patient described Ativan as somewhat helpful in cutting these "meltdowns" short by inducing sleep. The patient said that sleep would not save her forever. To hug her would have been unprofessional.

The patient's daytime sedation and low motivation began to interfere with her studies. As a result, we added Ritalin as needed in order to allow her to complete her senior year schoolwork. Although insufflation is always a concern when prescribing psychostimulants to mentally ill patients, I had to disregard any far-out notions about what abuses she might be doing to the linings of her nostrils in favor of keeping the sheen on her GPA.

The patient witnessed an episode of elevated mood and confidence. As a result, we made a decision to discontinue Lexapro and add Lamictal. After a difficult month-long titration period, during which the dosage was increased in weekly intervals of 25 mg, the patient improved and returned to baseline affect and function.

Every other week of the winter, the patient crossed campus in maroon plaid flannel pants with the hems worn and torn and stained with snow. The patient collected hooded sweatshirts and wore them under a puffy coat. I did not notice that the patient had lost 35 pounds and become underweight until she informed me.

We began to reduce Wellbutrin with the aim of discontinuing it, as we continued to be concerned about the likelihood of the patient having a bipolar spectrum disorder. Her original diagnosis of unipolar depression was based on her answers to questions asking that she catalog her moods at that moment. This method of scoring darkness has its limitations. For example, it asks that the college students we treat—most of whom are paying tens upon tens of thousands of dollars to take classes they report to be "fucking lame" in order to earn degrees that often prepare them for prestigious unpaid internships—sit in a waiting room and circle numbers on sheets fastened to a clipboard that correspond to statements like, "1.) I don't feel I am being punished. // 2.) I feel I may be punished. // 3.) I expect to be punished. // 4.) I feel I am being punished." We add up the numbers and decide whether we believe the students feel hopeless. We decided that the patient hated herself. We diagnosed her with "severe unipolar depression." While that was true at that moment, in other moments, she thought she was a rapper so famous she didn't need the ability to rap. The patient's apparent hypomania, associated with the use of antidepressant monotherapy, as well as known mood instability in bipolar patients resulting from antidepressant monotherapy (meaning, putting a bipolar patient on antidepressants will send them into ultradian [multiple cycles per day] cycling), led us to discontinue.

The patient's level of composure and charisma during office visits made it difficult to believe she was so fucked up.

After Lamictal was increased to 125 mg, the patient's mood regained stability. However, the patient developed a fever of 103, followed by a rash on the torso, upper arms, and legs, indicating that the patient may have developed Stevens-Johnson Syndrome, a rare and potentially fatal reaction. The patient would have been in the less-than-one percent of all patients on Lamictal who develop SJS.

The patient visited my office, stating that there was an emergency. After I closed the door, the patient lifted her shirt to reveal a rash on her stomach. The patient twisted her spine to show a rash on her back. For the first time, she cried in my office. "I know I have to stop taking it," the patient said, "or I'll die, but I don't want to stop taking it." I said, "I've never seen this before. Of all the people, I wish it didn't have to be you. Dammit, why did this have to happen to one of my favorite people?" When I said "people," I must have meant "patients." I had to send the patient downstairs for a benadryl injection that would knock her out until she would be kicked out of the clinic at closing time.

We were forced to discontinue Lamictal.

We added lithium. Once again there was improvement on 600 mg of lithium, with a resulting lithium level of 0.6 mEq/L, in the normal range.

The patient's hair kept getting shorter. Gold highlights the size of sunfish were added.

In May of 2007, the patient once again reported an episode of dysphoria with decreased social judgment. Lithium was increased to 900 mg.

The patient described a recent episode in which she had a lesbian encounter against a bathroom door and an encounter with a former partner on the lawn of a coffeehouse. The patient said, "Don't write that down. Just put, like, 'Manic shit going down.'" The patient could never make mental notes off-limits. When she once said hello to me outside the clinic, I pretended I didn't know who she was.

In June of 2007, the patient had another episode of elevated mood, increased alcohol consumption, negative self-reflection, and a sense of hopelessness. The patient said it was getting hard to take out the recycling, and bags of beer bottles accumulated under the kitchen table. At this point we added 10 mg of Abilify. There was some insomnia and akathisia, for which we added 1 mg of Klonopin nightly.

The patient said that her internal organs felt as if they were being constantly unraveled and knitted into something too tight. The patient said that her brain was uncoiling and re-clenching, as her fist does during a blood draw. The patient said she was determined to stay on Abilify. This was her attitude when I last treated her, before her move from Maryland to New Jersey to Washington upon graduation and entrance to graduate school.

The clinical picture is compatible with a mixed, rapid-cycling bipolar disorder. I missed her a lot when she left.

In conclusion, the patient's mood has been frequently and episodically unstable. There have been episodes of depression, as well as mixed and hypomanic symptoms. There have been ten-degree nights in ten-inch skirts, nights spent going through the Ativan rations while trying to sleep under a window left open to let the murderers in, nights racking up every point on every inventory and dreaming up new ones—the Washuta Online Spending Inventory, Identification with Famous Rappers Inventory, and Facebook Posts about Self-Worth Inventory. There have been nights when she genuinely believed she could really do the rest of her life, and nights when she really thought that no drug company was ever going to make a pill that could even lessen her pain. It kills me to know that she thinks this during most of her daily activities.

Although the patient's current course of Abilify has stabilized her mood, she does meet the criteria for bipolar disorder, mixed, rapid cycling, and will need to receive lifelong drug treatment. If anyone tells her otherwise and tells her to shrug it off and cheer up, I have promised her I will personally kick his or her teeth in. I wish Miss Washuta the best.

Sincerely,
The Psychiatrist[1]

---

[1] With edits from Elissa Washuta, 11/13/2007.

Next psychiatrist's postscript: The patient's akathisia, described as a constant feeling of agitation and unrest, intensified immediately after her move to Seattle. There, because no one in his right fucking mind should prescribe Abilify, that and Klonopin were discontinued and Seroquel was added. After adding 5 mg Lexapro, the patient achieved stability.

A Cascade Autobiography

PART 3

When I tell people I'm Native, they often ask, "How much?" It seems to be a reflex, the way, when I'm asked how I'm doing, I always fib that I'm "fine." I don't know why anyone cares to know my quantum, but I never want to be rude. I am three-thirty-seconds Indian: one-sixteenth Cascade and one-thirty-second Cowlitz. Since the Cascade tribe has been split into pieces, I am enrolled Cowlitz. When the Cascade leaders were hanged, all the other Cascade Indians were rounded up by Lieutenant Phil Sheridan, put on an island, and told that they would be shot if they tried to leave. You know Sheridan because you've heard, "The only good Indian is a dead Indian." He was talking about me because he was talking about Indians like my great-great-great-grandpa Tumalth, whom he hanged on March 28, 1856.

Tumalth was survived by his wives and daughters. Mary Wil-wy-i-ty, or Indian Mary, is the daughter whose blood eventually became mine. If you're asking me who the Indian was that made me Indian, I guess you're asking about Mary, because she was the last fullblood in my family line. Her second husband Louis, Abbie's dad, was Cowlitz. He was born to Lucy Skloutwout, a Lower Cowlitz woman whose descendants fill many chairs at council meetings. Mary was a very young girl when her dad died. Her sister Whylick Quiuck, or Virginia, was about nine at the time. When their dad was hanged, those little girls were enslaved, and the world was upended, never to be set right again.

Please Him

For eight years, the teachers at my Catholic grade school stuffed my skull with anything that would fit, starting with phonics (kindergarten), then quickly pressing in the history of the Revolutionary War (first grade), the corporal works of mercy (second), long division (third), Lenape history (fourth), human reproduction (fifth), cell biology (sixth), and sentence diagramming (seventh). My dad's Catholic school education had been structured but thorough, and my parents wanted to place me in a setting where my growing brain could absorb multitudes.

Our teachers challenged us to retain as much as possible. Our brains were empty vessels with stretchable walls. Every day, I was sent home with a backpack so heavy that I developed chronic back pain at age eleven, and my doctor suggested that I carry my textbooks in a rolling suitcase, a proposal I rejected. I didn't need help becoming any more of a freakish nerd than I already was.

In seventh grade, my best friend and I filled a notebook with nasty comments about our classmates and teachers, and a mean girl discovered it. I apologized profusely to the teachers and vice-principal. My parents, teachers, and the vice-principal agreed that after seven years at the school, I still couldn't fit in, so it was in my best interest to move on. I always say I got kicked out of Catholic school, because it sounds better than the truth: I had to throw in the towel because nobody liked me.

I failed while I excelled, learning the Ave Maria, Angelus, Apostle's Creed, and Nicene Creed by brain but not heart, because at some point, I became devoted to memorizing sex tips from *Cosmopolitan*. My impure heart ached, not for the Lord, but for something even glossier than prayer cards. *Cosmo* was full of good tips I needed to know about if I was going to be good in bed and worthy of love. I knew that sex could happen at any time, with anyone, and I had to be ready to please any man who might have me. My glasses saw through the atmosphere. Children, we were told over and over, are little lambs, are vessels, are innocents not yet spoiled by the world. As a child, I was charged with the task of keeping my soul pristine as I grew. Around me, I saw fiery souls, angry souls, souls already dying. Mine began to oxidize as it touched the stale New Jersey air.

THE COMMANDMENTS I PICKED UP ALONG THE WAY

1. I am the LORD your God. You shall not have strange gods before me.
2. Sister Agnes is always right and premarital sex is always a sin, because human bodies are made to advance God's will through making families.
3. You will never snag a husband if you don't know what to do with his dick. You learn this at twelve but still do not know anything else about dicks.
4. When it comes to your guy's penis, remember three things: If it's small, say it's the perfect fit. If it's average, say it's huge. If it's huge, he'll already know, but he'll still love hearing you say it anyway.
5. Say this: You are great, O Lord, and greatly to be praised. Great is your power and your wisdom is without measure.
6. Too many women can't admit when they're wrong, so letting him know when he's right, no matter what the topic is, will score you major points with him.
7. Penance requires the sinner to endure all things willingly, be contrite of heart, confess with the lips, and practice complete humility and fruitful satisfaction.
8. If you have to ask him if he enjoys giving you oral sex, then you have your answer: he doesn't. He might enjoy it more if he knew you'd be going down on him in return.
9. Touch him "down there" just like this (see illustration), touch his nipples, don't forget his sack, try out his nerve-packed pleasure button (ask first), use ice, blow, suck, not too cold, not too hot, put your thumb

QUESTIONS FROM COSMO THAT STARTED TO SEEM IMPORTANT WHEN I WAS TWELVE, EIGHT YEARS BEFORE I LOST MY VIRGINITY

Q. My guy wants me to tie him up. Exactly what do I do once he's bound to the bed?

Q. My boyfriend likes it when I touch his butt during sex. Should I go further?

Q. My dude wants me to talk dirty. Where do I start?

Q. My guy often spanks me when we're going at it. Does he want me to do it to him?

Q. My boyfriend has joked about threesomes. Do you think he wants to try it out?

Q. How come men always want to try anal sex?

A. You'd better do what he wants, or he might dump you.

Q. Am I normal down there?

Q. Will I become loose if I have too many partners?

Q. If I don't have sex for a while, will my vagina tighten up?

Q. Am I the right size?

A. Your smell is normal, unless you smell like fish, garbage, carrion, perfume, douches, meadows, or insecurity. And there is no right size for your va-jay-jay, unless you're so loose he can tell he's not your first, even though he knows he's not your first. Better do your Kegels: five sets of one hundred daily. Do them while you're cooking. Meanwhile, stop worrying: insecurity is such a turn-off. Focus on getting him hot instead.

Q. And what about him, is he normal?

Q. Is it weird for his penis to be darker than the rest of him?

right on that and your index finger right over there, make an "S" motion, make a kissing motion, a whispering motion, try humming, try ninety degrees, forty-five, show him your body, make figure eights or circles with your hips, squeeze your PCs in rhythm, let him see you, smell good, look good, do your squats and lunges, lose your love handles, watch basketball with him, do your Kegels, smile, look like you're having fun, make guacamole for the game but remember that a cup contains a whopping 367 calories, be as casual as possible, *definitely* don't forget his sack.

10. Men want a woman who loves sex and isn't afraid to sample new things. Men want you to be open to experimentation in the bedroom when they suggest it, but they don't necessarily want you to initiate wilder moves. Proposing anything that may appear choreographed can give them the impression that you've tried doing that with lots of other guys.

11. God is love; has an unlimited capacity for love; loves all, even sinners; answers all prayers; forgives; beckons; never plays games; never plays rough; asks for faith; has no form that you can see or touch. Nothing you can do can make God stop loving you.

12. Know that you are only here for one thing: God created everything for man, but man in turn was created to serve and love God and to offer all creation back to him.

13. Have faith.

Q. What if it's curved?

Q. Are his balls too small?

Q. He's kind of veiny, does that mean something?

Q. How many erections per day should he be having?

Q. Why is he less hard sometimes, does that mean he's not into me?

Q. Is he too small?

Q. Is he too big?

Q. Why are his balls so big?

A. It's all normal, and even if it's not, you had better not say anything.

Q. My boyfriend wakes up with eye crusties. Why?

A. He may be sleeping with his eyes open. You can help by assuring him you aren't going to judge his manhood in his sleep. Before you go to bed at night, get on your knees beside the bed, fold your hands, and tell him he's the best, the biggest, the hottest, the smartest, the most symmetrical, the least veiny, the most average-balled, the biggest-dicked, the most virile, and that crusty eye problem should be gone in no time.

Q. When I'm feeling all alone, where is God to help me?

Q. Why won't the guy I'm seeing call/text me back?

A. God is everywhere. Your guy is probably sick of you or fucking someone else. Back off and you might be able to win him back.

A(2). Or, you could back off, forget about him, and win your dignity back.

Q. But that's really fucking hard.

Sister Agnes, my sixth-grade teacher, shocked us into absorption and repentance. She told us she loved having her period because it was a gift from God. She projected hand-drawn fetuses onto the pull-down sheet over the blackboard. Every day of sixth-grade religion class, we took Bibles off a cart and readied ourselves for random Sword Drills (our Bibles being our swords in the fight against sin) during the lesson: she would call out a book, chapter, and verse, and we would look it up. The first to find the passage would read aloud. I desperately wanted to be fastest and read God's words back to Him. I was good at learning and memorizing. I was afraid of judgment coming, first from the Lord, then from the men, and I did what I could to prepare myself. I studied and waited for the afterlife. My belief in Christ and the Virgin pressed against every fiber of my green plaid jumper as I grew.

When I was in grade school, my confessions always came out the same. Bless me, Father, for I have sinned. My last confession was a month ago. I fought with my brother and disobeyed my parents and I took the Lord's name in vain. Penance: say some prayers. Absolved. I was generally honest in confession, but I never wanted to tell the priest that I made my Barbies have sex with each other (sometimes girl-on-girl, even) so I left that out. My last confession took place ten years ago. I have broken most of the commandments many times, as have most adults I know, but I haven't killed, haven't stolen, and in my mind this makes me a good person. But to God, I am not good.

The Old Testament bursts with a magic we had to accept as true. I learned to expect the formula: an angel appears, a child is born. This one must not cut his hair. He will save the Israelites. He plans a strategic marriage, part of the plan of the Lord, and is attacked by a lion on the way to propose. Of course he kills it; he is Samson. He flies into rages. He gives away his bride like a heifer. Hip and thigh, he slaughters the Philistines, kills more later with a donkey's jawbone. Samson smites, Samson rules, Samson leads Israel.

And then another woman. This one wants to know his secret. Don't they always, the people you get with? Want to know your secret, I mean, want to know what got you all fucked up and angry. Samson, stronger than I am, won't tell. So Delilah binds him to the bed with bowstrings. But how can a woman like Delilah tie down a man like Samson? With her charms; that's how she coaxes out his secret. She has a servant cut his hair. The Philistines burn out his eyes. When they enslave him, they emasculate him. Then his hair grows. He's out for blood. He shakes the pillars of the temple and dies with the Philistines when it crumbles. God said to do it. Love thy neighbor? Slaughter thy neighbor. And what of Delilah? She did it for money. As good a reason as any. Temptress, snake, bitch. Whatever. She got paid. She got out alive.

> Sister Agnes knew all the good prayers. A few times a week, she took us to the tiny in-school chapel to pray in place of a religion lesson. We would pray out loud together for a while, and then in silence. Sister said that already scripted prayers, like Hail Mary or Novenas, were the best, because whoever wrote them knew exactly what God wanted to hear. The Our Father was penned by Jesus himself, so you knew it was a real winner. I had a hard time staying conscious in that stuffy room, on my knees. One day I came so close to passing out, but I knew God would be displeased with me if I sat back. My best friend whispered, "Breathe in, breathe out, breathe in, breathe out. Like the Bush song." I never quite passed out in there. Back then, God loved me so much.

The four great virgin martyrs of the early Church are Lucy, Agnes, Agatha, and Cecilia. I always pictured them as slender-faced women with flaxen hair, their bodies swallowed by yards of cloth, their tiny, crushable features lit up by circular halos stationed behind their heads. Each saint looked exactly like any other, and their stories were difficult to distinguish, too, each one blending astounding piety with unspeakable violence: repeated failures to chop off Cecilia's head, the de-breasting of Agatha, the piercing of Lucy's eyes with a fork. Agnes, at age twelve or thirteen, was dragged naked through the streets of Rome to a brothel, where she was to be de-virginized so she could be lawfully executed according to Roman policy of the day. Some say she grew a coat of hair as she prayed, a heavenly defense mechanism; others say the men who attempted rape were blinded. An attempt to burn her at the stake was unsuccessful. The beheading, however, worked.

> While I learned so much about girls who died with their virginity intact, I never heard a word about male saints' virginity. In the Catechism, nuns' virginity is called for, while priests are asked only to be celibate—virginity isn't mentioned. Christian history is peppered with virgin martyrs who appeared after the Roman period, such as Joan of Arc and Maria Goretti, known for their unique stories. Sister Agnes was obsessed with Maria Goretti, the little saint who was murdered at the age of twelve by a young man whose advances she had spurned. Maria Goretti was to be a model for us girls: die before you open your legs and disappoint the Lord.

Sister told us a story about her guardian angel. Once, when Sister was a young woman, not yet a nun, a man followed her into a gas station bathroom. Her guardian angel made him disappear, somehow. I imagined her with long, dark hair and jeans, with a happier face, maybe even makeup. I imagined what she wasn't really saying:

> Her new life was the product of a furious twisting, a repulsive stroking of thighs. The shadow of a man's hands rose up the bathroom stall door as she struggled with the lock and tried to breathe. Years later, hidden behind a convent's brick walls, embraced by the arms of her new vocation, she kneeled on the maroon tile floor with a bucket and rags and scrubbed. She learned to avert her eyes with humility, begged God to make her selfless, closed her eyes and felt her spine roll under the world's sorrow. She memorized chaplets and

novenas but could not turn away from the stare of the angry eyes that penetrated walls. In her room—a cell, they called it—she asked God to take her in her sleep.

Maria Goretti, born 1890, martyred 1902, patron saint of rape victims, was, alongside fetuses, Sister Agnes's object of most intense devotion. When Maria was twelve, as she sat on the veranda of a barn at her parents' farm, some neighbor boy of twenty tried to get her to bring him to her bedroom. Of course she refused. So he dragged her, he tried to rape her, she fought, he stabbed. Fourteen times. Then he left. She bled out, but not to death, not quite; death came the next day in a hospital bed. Last words: she forgave the guy and prayed that God would, too. The guy went to prison for thirty years. Maria's mother lived to attend her daughter's canonization. The rapist became a Franciscan. He died with a picture of Maria on his nightstand.

Sister Agnes said we were supposed to live by Maria Goretti's example. We were supposed to cross our legs, clamp them shut with steel; we were supposed to guard our chastity with our lives. It made sense. My body was a book of rules, my heart the spine, my skin plastered with pages. Written on each one was the text that held the world together. Do not steal. Do not lie, swear, disobey. Do not get angry. Don't even let your thoughts go bad or the poison will fill your veins. Above all, do not fuck.

When the nuns found out I was Cowlitz Indian, they offered me Blessed Kateri Tekakwitha, the Lily of the Mohawks, as a spiritual guide. I knew nothing more than that she was holy and that I was to ask her to speak to the Lord on my behalf. On prayer cards, she was rendered with deep honey skin and delicate, anglicized features. Behind her twin braids shone the circular halo that adorned the heads of all saints. She was Indian and I was Indian, so the nuns thought I would respond to her. They never told me about the smallpox scars that disfigured and half-blinded her, Mohawk accusations of sorcery and promiscuity in response to her conversion, or her self-mortification practices that included whips, hair shirts, iron girdles, and beds of thorns. Kateri—no, Catherine, post-conversion—could withstand up to twelve hundred self-induced lashes at a time. Prolonged fasting brought clarity. Hot coals brought her closer to God. While Kateri's bloodletting had once taken traditional Mohawk forms, Jesuit priests supplied all the instruments of self-ravage that a good Catholic girl might need to purify her dark Native heart.

In 1680, at the age of twenty-four, Catherine died a virgin. The old Kateri was long gone, and miraculously, so were the scars that had once marked her face, now perfectly pale.

I could not pray to Kateri Tekakwitha. She seemed more like one of my Native American Barbies than a saint. With her braids and ethnically confused features, her prayer card image reminded me enough of myself that I found it impossible to venerate her. Kateri could not be trusted to do any better than I could with my desperate implorations to the Lord.

> Prayer is not a satisfying outlet: you talk to God, God doesn't answer; you have to have faith that his plan is in action, and you pray some more. I used to pray to saints instead of God because if I didn't get what I wanted, I could blame heavenly miscommunication. I prayed novenas to Saint Jude, patron of hopeless causes, asking him to make the cross-eyed boy I loved love me back. It never worked. I was like a *before* girl in a teen movie, gangly with bad bangs and glasses, no concept of style, no sense of how to present the new body I was sprouting. The boys joked about my undesirability, one telling me that another had dedicated a love song to me on the radio or was going to put a note into my locker later. The nuns promised that in heaven, we would eternally appear as we had at our hottest in life, but I ran out of patience. I lost faith sometime near the end of sixth grade. God had so many people working so hard to make him happy that I knew

he wouldn't miss me when I was gone from his flock. Anyway, the nuns had told me that Jesus loved me unconditionally, so I wasn't worried about making any effort to try to snag him.

The summer after seventh grade, I bought my first pair of black plastic, modified Buddy Holly glasses, a new wardrobe, and makeup, ready to reinvent myself and broadcast a message to my new classmates, who didn't know the bookish girl I had been at All Saints Regional: *you don't know me, but I am very freaking cool.*

To be a sinful woman is to be a whore. The New Testament never says so, but Mary Magdalene has a reputation. Woman's sin is sexual. So, even though there is no biblical evidence of Mary Magdalene's sluttiness, we believe that it is so. Mary Magdalene and Jesus were tight, leading scholars to speculate. All that we know about her is what we place into the marginal white space in the New American Bible. Even if she wasn't a prostitute in life, she sure is a hooker now: see *The Last Temptation of Christ, Jesus Christ Superstar,* and *The Passion of the Christ.* Mary sits in heaven with her hair down past her shoulders, among the girls whose breasts are just beginning to grow, whose hymens still guard the span of the chastity they died for. Mary lived to see her body break and heal, to change over years, to become immaterial. She lived to see God die. In heaven she feels no need to cross her legs at the knee.

Mary of Egypt, patron saint of penitents, is likely the slut earlier Catholic scholars confused with Mary Magdalene. Just as Mary Todd Lincoln shouldn't be confused with Mary-Kate Olsen, Mary of Egypt was a separate woman from a different time with a different agenda. I never learned about her in Catholic school—maybe because she wasn't important, maybe because keeping track of so many women named Mary was too much to ask of schoolchildren, maybe because she made it okay to sleep around as long as penance eventually comes. Born around 344, died around 421, Mary moved to Alexandria at age twelve and started sleeping around. She didn't fuck for the money, she said; she wanted it, loved it, couldn't get enough of the cock. So she went to Jerusalem for the Feast of the Exaltation of the Holy Cross. It was an anti-pilgrimage: she wasn't looking for salvation, she was cruising the pilgrims. Something happened—visions, forces—and she repented. She crossed the Jordan River to live like a beast in the desert. When Saint Zosimas found her, she was naked, more animal than human, clairvoyant. She could walk on water. I try to explain this away with what I know: petit mal seizures, maybe, because I can't believe in superpowers. Zosimas left and returned to find her dead. With the help of a passing lion, he buried her.

In 1 Kings and 2 Kings, Jezebel, Phoenician queen of Israel, is manipulative, scheming, idolatrous, and powerful, but never a slut. Like Mary Magdalene, she has become a slut in our eyes millennia after her story first emerged, but since she worshipped Baal and never the LORD God, her redemption can only be secular and feminist: she was so strong she made her husband's knees buckle, made pagans of the Israelites. A woman only has power to make a nation of men fall if she has evil, a force stronger than nearly anything, working through her. Somehow, when she was turned from Bible story to pure myth, she became an adulteress who turned the Israelites into sexual deviants. Mary Magdalene's sin was personal; Jezebel infected a nation. What a woman! I thought. Sister said, "Pray against the spirit of Jezebel." Each night, I said a rosary in bed, counting pearls, sometimes following it up with the Angelus, even though I knew that prayer was only said at certain times of day, hoping that nobody would mind. Afterward, I would try to think happy thoughts, as my dad had told me to do when I was afraid to sleep, and then I'd try a Regina Coeli or Salve Regina, and more happy thoughts, but eventually, I ran out of happy thoughts and rote-memory prayers, and I thought of regal Jezebel, and of Mary Magdalene hanging with God and the boys so easily, and I'd sometimes drift off thinking that someday, I could wake up being a woman who rules the world.

As my primary and secondary school years passed, and I counted the hours until college, my longing turned to acute craving, to something like a nutrient deficiency I could feel in my body. In high school, I would finally take on a boyfriend. Jake and I dated for three years, into college, but he wasn't my perfect love, even though he often gave me flowers, gifts, and handmade cards. We regularly professed our love for one another, and at first, I did mean it, but at sixteen, I wasn't prepared to keep meaning it for so long.

In that virginal space, in which my flesh had no saintly reason for abstinence, my desperation took the form of a sort of ugly love medicine. I longed to touch someone whom I really wanted. I had my opportunity to lose my v-card to Jake, but I just couldn't do it—he had become too much like a family member. I still thought I meant it when I told him I loved him, but it was a kind of love that even the nuns would have been comfortable with.

Eventually, when I was a college sophomore, I summoned up the resolve to break up with him. I knew it would hurt him—worse, because I was his world, in a way that I could no longer handle. He asked for a two-month extension. I considered it, at first, but then let myself go. By then, my limbs fit my torso, my haircut fit my face, and I didn't need to study *Cosmo*'s glossy secrets to trick boys into liking me. I wielded phenomenal powers. I went too far, too fast; knew too much, too soon. A few years later, curious friends and even boys whose hands were wedged between my waistband and pelvis would ask me, "How many have you had?" as if they wanted to see whether I was okay to drive. It was a question of the very young adults, those who want to know how their numbers measure up. Mine began to feel like a statistical outlier, eventually, because I had been so terrified of the burden of sainthood, the pain of my torment, and I tried to lance my wound, but I cut deeply, and, calling it sacrifice, calling it progress, kept cutting.

A Cascade Autobiography

PART 4

When I was five, my kindergarten teacher split the class into Pilgrims and Indians with construction paper costumes to teach us about our national heritage; my parents had explained to me that I was Indian, and the classroom taught me what that meant. When I was six, my dad taught me how to spell "Cowlitz," and I wrote it at the bottom of my drawings. When I was seven, I became obsessed with mermaids, certain that I could fuse my legs into a fin if I pressed them together firmly enough under my modest sub-desk plaid. At eight, I created dioramas of buildings where other Native people's ancestors slept, and though the teacher told me this was my heritage, I was not certain that I believed in cacti or mesas, having never seen them.

Faster Than Your Heart Can Beat

Imagine a vise,
Martin says, in which you are both
the thing being held
and what holds it in place, metal
grinding on metal, that shining embrace.

ENID SHOMER, "MY FRIEND WHO SINGS BEFORE BREAKFAST"

Only penetration counts. I never let them stretch me for good, I remain virginally tight. Of course I keep a tally. Each addition proves that I am not afraid to repeat my mistakes until one of my decisions happens to be good. Counting backwards is a must.

#24. You might be a hologram. I might be psychotic, conjuring up the deep wells above your clavicle, your lips ten times softer than the skin inside my wrists, your hair the color of the gold that hangs from my neck and ears when I want to gleam. I never even asked for you. I would not have known what to ask for, could not have imagined the strong arch of your eyebrows. I don't even have to ask you to take it slow. "How am I so lucky?" you ask. "How am I so lucky?" I ask. People want to know whether you're my boyfriend, officially. I want to know whether you're real.

You're not. Two months in, we break up in my car. I draw a graph in the air: my affection started down here and went up, but you started at the same place and plummeted down; I end with my index fingers in the air, pointing at nothing. I cry for two days. Two weeks later, sitting with good friends on rocky Alki Beach in West Seattle, I take pictures of my pastel high-tops. In the bright sunlight we're finally seeing lately, I see every pore on the lavender leather, and I see my shiny shin pores, and I know that I'll start to forget you soon, but I couldn't dump myself if I tried.

#23. My best friend broke up with you months ago. She has granted me permission to add you to my list. Months after you two stop being civil, I go over to your apartment and step around the jumble of the possessions you aim to sell before migrating south.

You say you cannot wait for the rebellion, that MDA is ecstasy's prettier cousin, that Bill Murray makes a better Hunter S. Thompson than Johnny Depp does, that you're really into this Native resistance in my blood, that my breasts are a nine point five out of ten. You want to know about her new boyfriend.

The sex is fine. The hugs are excellent, exactly what I was looking for, what I bartered access to my insides for. We are alike, unsure of ourselves but inflated by the blustery notions we stuff inside our chests to keep us from caving in. You define your identity by what you are counter to; I define mine by my voids.

Long after you've left town, my friend and I drunkenly conduct a year-in-review of what we've been up to and how our tallies have swelled. Astonished that we didn't mind sharing dick, she says, "We're kinda like Mormon wives now."

#22. I want you more than I have ever wanted any bartender. I see you twice a week at karaoke. Your Acqua di Gio, cologne of choice of frat boys, pokes into my scent memory. We flirt for weeks while I watch you charm the customers; we have a couple of platonic-feeling dinners that I wish were real dates, and I learn that you hate the bar, hate flirting with men for tips, but the unspoken truth is that you're not skilled at much and your body is compact and hard. I tell you I'm going to teach you about how to write essays for your community college class, but instead, we get trashed, and you take me home. You do me for five hours. We only rest when you go outside in your boxer-briefs and piss on your neighbors' house. You keep doing me long after my vadge turns to baguette crust. When you slur that you love me, I tell you to shut up and come.

I tell you I am taking your studded belt, and if you want it back, you will come to my place soon. All the bar patrons have seen the belt circling your waist like Saturn's rings. This trophy lies on my bedroom floor while you tell me, twelve hours later, via text, that you made a mistake that we should never speak of again; while I drive around at night, wishing I had never been born; while I give you my order at the bar and pretend, for your sake, that we have never met.

In a few months we are pals again. On the bar's anniversary night, I pass by as the fleet of bartenders and bar-backs gather on the sidewalk for a photo. You wear cross-trainers with your tux, like a boy going to prom, and for the first time, all my attraction is gone, and I almost love you like a sister would.

When you tell me that you got so mad at your girlfriend that if you were gay and she were a dude you would have hit her for sure, I have to stop with the love.

#21-18. During my first long Seattle winter, you men come and go like customers at the café where I work. None of you have last names. You have Prince Albert piercings and shaved body parts. You crumple my dress into a ball, try to tear it off me, or lay it over an end table. You buy me drinks and steal my credit card. You dwell in trashy bars and sometimes my quiet bedroom. You leave suck marks, bruises, and scratches on my body; shriveled condoms on my floor. Your faces blend together like melted plastic. I meet you without well-formed expectations, giving you nothing to rise to.

I tell friends half-truths about being stable now that I am in Seattle and on the right meds. I say I have some issues left to work out. I do not usually say that this entails straddling strangers.

In my East Coast circles, random sex was never really random, and nobody ever used the word *anonymous*, but in Seattle, I can absorb every one-night stand into my body and keep it there. Once I bring you into my home or cautiously enter yours, then exit, I can avoid seeing you ever again, having failed to get what I was looking for. What do I get out of this? I don't know. If I knew, I would find somewhere else to get it.

#17. For my twenty-third birthday, two days after Thanksgiving, most of my friends are out of town and unavailable to celebrate, so I decide to settle for a one-night stand and a back rub. A friend and I go to a hipster bar where sombreros and fake flowers decorate the ceiling. Over dinner earlier, she told me I am good at making sultry eyes, so I practice this tonight. I catch your attention. You buy me a drink, and I invite you home. I have condoms and lube beside my bed, and you say I am very well prepared. After my back rub, we have quick missionary sex. Afterward, in the bathroom, I find blood on the toilet paper, blood on the condom, just a little. This is not my period. Not since my first time have I bled like this.

At seven, you ask for directions to the bus stop. We avoid exchanging numbers. We don't kiss goodbye. We smile and say, "See you later," even though we won't. All day I feel strange about how good the downstairs door sounded when it shut behind you, and how much I believed your kind goodbye smile. In my apartment, there is no trace of you but the shriveled, reddened condom; you never existed.

#16. Saturday morning, Halloween weekend, I stroll through the farmers' market on your arm, dressed in a naughty nurse costume, a winter coat, and a pair of Nikes. In the car I point out the mountains, now snow-capped, and you tell me about being a toddler in Siberia and tunneling through deep snow. You are an electrical engineering graduate student, a member of a research group; you are the first man I have slept with who has his shit together. When I realize this, I feel silly and cheap, and in the skimpy nurse costume, I am. You tell me you will see me again, but not during the week because you cannot afford the distraction. I wish I had a change of clothes. I wonder whether I should be hopeful when you hold my hand; I wonder whether my neck is covered in bite marks from last night. As it turns out, I shouldn't be hopeful; you never left a mark.

#15. On our third date I summon the courage to ask your last name, but I still do not ask your age. You say you walk with your hips forward because it makes walking easier. When I first saw you stacking glasses behind the bar at the Crescent, I was quite sure I would never rip off all your clothes. I was right: we strip separately, me, then you.

When you end it, you admit that you are thirty-four, as though it's nothing that you are twelve years my senior. In the months after, we see each other a few times around Seattle and pretend we never met. When I see you on a bus, I sit across the aisle from you, never turning my head to look. My peripheral vision provides glances of your leather sneaker on your knee, your green knit cap, but no explanations of what I was lacking, what in me could make you turn to stone when you look back at me.

Months later, I will duck into a used video game store near the University and see you behind the counter. While I browse in silence, I think of your dump of a place, your college-hippie-chic tapestry covering your bedroom's French doors to offer privacy from your roommate, your mattress on the floor. There was no lack in me; there was nothing more than my tendency to choose the grit-coated seraphs out of whom I had no business trying to force love.

I leave without buying anything, say, "Thank you," and never see you again.

#14. We meet at a Melvins show downtown, and you kiss me too much, too publicly. I have a yeast infection but a girl cannot tell a boy she has a yeast infection, so I let every thrust hurt badly. When I drive you home to the other side of Seattle, you point at the broad, white horizon and say, "The mountains are out."

#13. My friend tells me that while I am in New Jersey, staying with my parents during the month before my move to Seattle, I have a mission to give you relief from your cunt of a girlfriend. I accept this. I have seen no photos of her, and you never mention her, so to me she does not exist. I try to put myself in her place, but I have never been in her place, so I do not try very hard.

You have hips like a lady and treat me like a girlfriend. You keep telling me you are old, twenty-six, as though I'm still hanging from a placenta at age twenty-two. If we go downstairs to my purse for a condom, your parents will wake up, but you swear to God, *swear to God* you're clean. I figure I am probably clean too, but you never ask.

You used to work at a pharmacy. In bed I tell you about my medications. A month ago, I started on antipsychotics for my bipolar disorder, but the drug is causing akathisia, a cocktail of anxiety, restlessness, and dread. There is something I can take, you say, but I do not believe that I will ever feel right again. This is my sixth psych drug, and it has stabilized me; chemical torture is the trade-off.

You ask me to leave silently. When I drive back to my parents' house, my temporary home between moves, and I roll down the window to ruffle your smoke out of my short hair, I become a disobedient child again. You live farther into the state than I've ever driven, deep in a patch of woods, and as I drive, I realize I know nothing about what you do with yourself out here, who you see, how you make the time pass between trips to the diner and household chores.

I have a long trip ahead of me. I speed; I am home by two.

A year later, I call you to say hello after too much red wine. You tell me that you tried to kill yourself: Xanax, Valium, codeine, and a bottle of red wine. It didn't work. I know about these things. I tell you how I would've done it.

#12. All my friends are drinking because I am about to leave Maryland for good. In the woods behind the party, you kiss me through a spider web. I am obsessed with the gap in your teeth. You have whiskey dick in my bed and say the feeling of my fingernails is inconsequential. I keep saying, "You're so hot, you're so hot," because I don't know how else to say that I don't even care about sex—I just want to stare at that gap in your teeth and listen to your voice rumbling over it. Once you get it up, I feel too bad to put a condom on it.

Two days later, I load my boxes into my dad's truck and unload them in New Jersey. In the month before my move, I separate proper adult clothes from ho gear and put the latter in boxes in the attic. Now I am an adult. I take Klonopin every night to sleep. Soon I will shed my old life like a cicada's brittle shell.

#11. You tell me it has been weeks since you smoked the last of your weed, smoked the resin you scraped off the bowl, and now that you have been laid off, you're too broke to get more. I will only see you because you aren't high tonight. When you are high, your limbs are everywhere, your words move faster than your heart can beat. In your basement bedroom, there is almost no room to move because of the two beds, one full-sized and one twin. You make the bed for me. It could be day or night. We never sleep; we emerge from under the earth to sit in your backyard swing and share cigarettes at twilight. Later, when I see you at a bar, I pretend there is nothing between us, and thinking of your mostly empty beds makes me hurt.

In the month before my move from Maryland, you attempt to make yourself a fixture so that I will have to keep thinking of you when I'm on the other side of the continent. I remain noncommittal. You put me in a bath when I drink so much my blood turns to liqueur. Later, after I move to Seattle and you move to L.A., we meet by the Pacific Ocean, kiss on beaches as bleached as I had imagined I'd find in somewhere called Malibu, and rub aloe on each other's sun-singed bodies. We decide to become a couple. A few months later, you visit Seattle and leave string cheese wrappers around my apartment. When you bring me to visit your rich relatives, who live in town, I flirt with your well-adjusted sixteen-year-old cousin, who keeps Strunk & White's *Elements of Style* next to his bed. He makes eyes at me over the dinner table like a grown man. With enough money, perhaps any child can seem like an adult. You're too old to be reformed from your full-mouthed chortling. While I watch you enjoy yourself, I wish I could raise you right.

I become a huge bitch. For much of your visit, I spend the hot July days out on my balcony, refusing to speak, while you paint at the dining room table in your blue-splattered boxers. You say you want to understand my bipolar disorder, but you are lying: you seem to be confusing "want to understand" with "want me to understand that I can will it away with some positive thinking." When we fuck, it hurts so much that my abdomen sobs, while my eyes betray nothing. Even my vagina has had enough of you. I don't know which is more terrifying: being loved or being asked to love.

We agree that we can't make it long-distance, an amicable split that keeps my smoky moods from smashing into your kaleidoscopic crayon-box brain. We've been out of touch for months when your mother calls to tell me she had you committed. She gives me the number for the mental health ward and the best hours to call. Over the phone, you tell me you don't believe the doctor when he says you're bipolar, like me; and you don't see why everyone is so upset that you've been expressing yourself by throwing books; and you just want everyone to let you be homeless. I tell you to take your meds and I realize how hard it must be to love me. The painting you made that week we sweated our skins off remains hidden in my closet. You're too broken with reality to want to talk about anything but the fact that all of this is perfectly normal, and even though I want to cradle your crazy brain in my arms and try to heal you with all the everyday magic I've conjured up since my own diagnosis, I must remind myself that you're far away, you're in good hands, and because I regularly exhaust my powers keeping myself on the outside of the institutional wall, I have to let myself off the hook.

#10. On your couch, you lean in close, take my hand, and pull my fingers so hard they might come out of their sockets. One by one, my knuckles crack. Your friend is lying on the floor; he cracks my toes, and then passes out.

In your bed, we're surrounded by your high school wrestling trophies. You haven't been competitive since you were eighteen and skinny. After a ten-minute rest, you want to go again, from behind. I bury my face in the pillow and do not have to look at you while I wonder how we got from friendship to this. I tell you it hurts and you say, just one more minute, almost there. You are wrong. After we finish you crack my knuckles again, and I tell you to stop it, there are no cracks left.

You agree to dose me with an Ambien. I graduated two weeks ago, and have nearly nothing to do with my time until I move, so I am prepared to sleep all day and hope you don't decide in the middle of the night that you're ready for more of me.

Weeks later, you want to take me out on a real date. Fancy Chinese dinner, French film, cocktails, strip club. The place is called "Good Guys" and one of the women looks like a racing dog, all ribs, but the others have a little fat on them. I tell you I could strip here and you say I am probably wrong. You give me dollars to wave at them and I already know I have to put out. On the way to my apartment, you order me to stuff my cold Chinese leftovers into your mouth. You lick my fingers clean. In bed, even though I don't believe in blue-balls, I don't challenge you.

You talk too much. I put on heavy metal and scratch your back with my fingernails. I attempt some gymnastics and stand over your prostrate body—once the compact form of a wrestler, now fleshy and weak—and my feet pin your elbows to the bed. "How do other guys handle this?" you ask. "How do they handle you?"

"I don't know," I reply, then amend it: "They don't, really."

#9. You eat me out on the dining room floor of your parents' house in the Baltimore suburbs while my best friend sleeps on the couch in the next room. You push your tongue into my mouth and say, "This is how you taste," as though you are the first to teach me this. In the morning, your parents ask you for your sleeping friends' full names. I am too afraid of them to walk past them to the bathroom, so I hold in my morning piss all the way home. Until I heard your voice cramp as your father gave you the third degree, you had seemed so adult, being a year out of college and much more self-assured than the rest of us, but like your sandy-eyed passengers, you're somebody's kid, tethered to the nest.

Early on, you make it clear that we are wrong for each other. You are looking for something, and I am not that thing.

Every time I sleep over, before bed, you fill two shot glasses with saline solution and label them left and right for my contact lenses, a gesture that I keep telling myself is just friendly, not boyfriendly, so that I won't start growing on you like mold. The nightly ritual is the best thing you ever do for me. The worst comes after you ask, "Wanna try something new?"

#8. I should have known you were bad news when you rolled out of bed, opened your top drawer, and showed off your handgun before you even took the condom off. The gun is in your glove box the night you come to my apartment, crush up my anxiety pills, and snort the powder. When my ex-boyfriend knocks on the window, you get jealous and pull a knife on me. After I throw you out, my friends lament the fact that I will never again ride in that BMW. Only one points out that I shouldn't have left my fingerprints on that gun.

#7. You finish in less than thirty seconds every time. I count. Afterward, you run to the bathroom and leave me alone for ten times the length of our fucking. You never admit I de-virginized you. You end it after a few weeks. I will miss your visits, our awkward questions about each other's days and goings-on posed from opposing armchairs before we would stand and work on an embrace. The problem with this, you say, is that I am not Jewish and you cannot marry me. I wonder whether it was the Virgin Mary nightlight and archangel candles in the bathroom that sent you packing. I want to tell you that I didn't mean it—not the countertop devotion, not the beneath-sheets detachment. I know you don't get a do-over of your first fuck. All I can do is let you go.

#6. I skip my psychiatrist appointment to go sneaker shopping with you. For weeks we sit on your porch, smoking, and you tell me you can feel your lungs dying. At my apartment, you finger me with a precision I have never known while you talk on the phone. Your best friend wants to know why we aren't at Starbucks yet, and you tell him, ten minutes. You get a few good thrusts in before you go soft, saying, "I guess I'm not really into girls." Because you keep your shirt on the whole time, I never really get to know your skin. For months, in my apartment, I see visions of you in the blueness of cloudy days. I see you across the table again, see you in the bathroom rolling off a condom. You stop talking to me; I try hard to stop loving you. The task is so difficult. You are the one who will tell me, "Girl, you need a fucking bottle of Xanax," who will hang up on my manic calls, and who will say you can't truly give two fucks because you have no soul. But you do have a soul, and when I look at you from just the right angle, I can see it sweat.

#5. You keep a gallon of lotion next to your bed and need me to keep hand cream next to mine. You insist that I have problems and need to get professional help. From where I'm lying, worn out and hurting, fucked raw, I see all kinds of problems that you don't. The problem is that I was devastated by someone else; the problem is that I refuse to walk down the block to get a smoothie without changing into a dress and high heels.

When I know we're nearing the end, I tell you in tears that I'm close to making myself lovable, and could maybe even start loving you, too, but you say I'm so far off. I wish I could tell you that I have even grown fond of the man-tits you've always tried to hide and exercise away, an aberration on your skinny frame, and the way your palms fly to your chest when you feel insecure, but now, I see only certainty in your face as you tell me that you've had enough.

After you ditch me and tell my secrets to the next girl, I tell everyone about your lotion-hungry dick; you tell the Internet I never get wet.

#4. Your fencing weapon is foil, mine is épée, so we never bout. I collect medals while you fail classes. I mark the number of times we fuck on an envelope full of our condom wrappers, which I keep in an unplugged mini-fridge. We get up to nine—nine nights that I watch for you to walk into my courtyard, nine nights you refuse to sleep beside me—before you drop out of school and leave me to go home to New York. I will wait for you to come back to your studies. You play around with the idea of re-enrolling, but never do. I plead, "I miss you so much, will you ever come back?" and you say, "I miss you too." My heart is stuck up in a tree, waiting for you to knock it down with a stick. I still quiver when I conjure up memories of my hands moving down the lengths of your muscles, and you still cannot understand why.

Just when I think I've convinced you that paradise is in me, you move to Florida, too far away to drive to me or think of me, with your sun-cooked brain trained on learning to fly planes. You finally start getting As and take on a serious girlfriend. In Facebook photos, your sweet tea body, losing the thin layer of baby beluga blubber you needed to keep out the Maryland cold, looks no more real to me than the palm trees that now appear around you in pixelated cell phone photos. I have never been to Florida, and I don't believe that anyone will turn me on again. My paradise is lost.

#3. You tell me sex is funny, and it's okay that my boyfriend is knocking on the window. You'll go.

#2. For twelve months we burrow into your apartment. We keep tallies of our fucking on snow days; we set up a tent on the bed and sweat on each other inside. Later you will bring other girls into the tent, but forever you will know you shouldn't.

We place one of my épées on the floor, jump over it, and declare ourselves married. You tell me that if I get sick of you, I will have to divorce you.

I am a good wife. When you drink yourself into the hospital, your stomach screaming, I ride in the ambulance because I have no car. The driver is reluctant to let me ride shotgun, but I tell him we have no one else around here, no family nearby, no friends. In the morning, when I am forced to leave the hospital, after you have been given a diagnosis of acute pancreatitis and enough Dilaudid to silence your gut, I take a ride from a stranger. After he drops his son off at school, he says he deals drugs, but not crack. When I shiver, he tells me he'll warm me up. He says I can do what I want, it's not like I'm married. . . . I arrive home safe, but you and I know that no matter what could have happened, someone else already ruined me anyway.

When things are good, we sit on the balcony and drink Kool-Aid and Everclear, smoking cigars. When things go badly, you ask me to put out a cigarette on your arm.

Weeks of nausea coincide with a late period and I make you drive me to the drugstore to buy a pregnancy test. I am not pregnant. The nausea stays for months. A radioactive tracer threaded into my veins, and through my gallbladder, tells doctors that the organ has stopped working. After I get it removed, I fall out of love with you; they might as well have excised my heart.

#1. I have given hand jobs, blow jobs. I have been eaten out and fingered. I have tried to fuck, but I was too dry and tight, and my high school boyfriend was too gentle to push. To be a virgin at twenty is to be in danger of being a virgin forever. My vagina feels sealed shut; even using tampons is impossible. So I tell you we have to take it slow. You are the last man to whom I say this.

You stand above me and jack off onto my belly and breasts. You demand that I blow you and that I immediately brush my teeth afterward. You want a naked sleepover. I agree to all these things. I do not agree to what comes after.

I get the morning-after pill at the university clinic. When I cannot stop crying, the doctor says that this boy may have taken advantage of me. I reply that she just doesn't know the complexities of this exact situation, and I take a handful of free condoms. I bleed all day.

When I get back into the bed that used to be for sleep, I play the scene over in my head, as though I could improve upon it in my thoughts. But still, in every remembering, in the middle of the night you are on top of me. Still, every time, I say no, you say yes, and to you, it is nothing but a difference of opinion.

A Cascade Autobiography

PART 5

When I was nine, in our New Jersey history class, we learned about the Lenni Lenape who had come before us. They seemed even further away than my own Indians because they had been right here, but the textbook said they were gone. When I was ten, a classmate told me she was Indian, too, and I said she was wrong, because she had never said so before. I wanted to be the only Indian around.

Preliminary Bibliography

VARIOUS PICTURE BOOKS ABOUT MERMAIDS.

As a small girl, I was not allowed to collect women's lingerie ads from the newspaper circulars, and I was told to clean out the images of the busty Jessica Rabbit from my desk, but I was never denied the pleasure of reading picture books about mermaids, whose breasts were cupped by seashells or draped with long hair. All the strange anatomy below the flat stomach and delightful navel was consumed by a fish's body. Fish, unlike breasts, I knew: my father gutted them at the hatchery every day for post-mortem diagnosis and sometimes kept their livers in the basement freezer for later study. For Halloween, twice, I was a mermaid, but I didn't really want to be one; I wanted to put my hands to them.

JUVENILE NONFICTION ABOUT SHARKS.

A shark could tear me apart. A shark is bigger than my bed, my bedroom, maybe my one-story house (before the addition). In the books there were photos of cages that were meant to protect divers from sharks. I saw a cage in a museum and understood: there is no protection from sharks.

JUVENILE NONFICTION ABOUT SHIPWRECKS.

Books about important shipwrecks adhere to the facts: how many passengers were on the *Titanic*, where the *Lusitania* went down. I could not fathom the thought of the bottom of the ocean, then. I pictured the ghostly remains of a sunken ship from *The Little Mermaid*; books adhered to the facts, but the unsaid truth had to be that mermaids swam between the rotting beams. I outgrew the books, but at thirteen I saw *Titanic* and cried because love always failed, and massive ships could sink, and Leo DiCaprio's face was too perfect to exist. Hollywood could not convince me that majestic ships could really go down like that; I had to grow up before I understood that smooth sailing means nothing. When Kate Winslet's land-mermaid body appeared naked on the screen, my friend asked me why I stared.

COLE, JOANNA. *ASKING ABOUT SEX AND GROWING UP.* **NEW YORK:**
MORROW JUNIOR BOOKS, 1988.

Is it normal to be curious about growing up? Is it okay to ask about sex? Yes and yes, but only at home. At school, the nun will talk about the silver chalice of adulthood that the man and his wife pull out of the lake.

Why are girls' and boys' bodies different? What sex organs does a girl have? Can a girl see her sex organs? What is the first change that happens to girls? How do breasts grow? Many of the line drawings, crafted by Alan Tiegreen, illustrator of Beverly Cleary's Ramona books, have taken a place in my memory as though they were real flesh instead of thin lines and blank space. I looked harder at the girl drawings: the modest breasts, mounds of pubic hair, stages of development. I was somewhere between the child picture and young woman picture, but somehow, even the adult breasts seemed not to have reached their potential in my comparison to the robust Jersey sets around me. What would I grow up to be?

Do kids ever have crushes on someone of the same sex? By the time I was reading the book, my girl-crushes were long gone, having given way to scrutiny, admiration, and comparison: crushing gone rotten.

Why do people have sexual intercourse? What is a virgin? Do people ever make love with people they don't know well?

What is sex abuse? What is rape? What is the difference between "okay touching" and sex abuse? How can kids protect themselves from sex abuse? What should you do if you are sexually abused?

Near the end, Cole writes, "The most important thing to know about sex as you grow up is to respect yourself and others" (85). I learned about tampons, testicles, umbilical cords, locker rooms, and ejaculation; why didn't her final message stick?

LAMB, WALLY. *SHE'S COME UNDONE.* **1992. REPRINT, NEW YORK: WASHINGTON**
SQUARE PRESS, 1996.

465 pages form an epic, a whole life, one much worse than mine. I was fourteen and my only problems were that my moods swung so violently that the guidance counselor insisted on seeing me weekly, thinking I was bipolar; and that my Internet boyfriend, Joey, threw a fit if I left the computer to go to the mall with my parents or to my grandparents' in the next township over. Dolores Price had real problems. I wanted to be raped, too, so people would know my pain was real and rooted. I escaped the computer

the summer after eighth grade to sit on the porch and read, listening to Radiohead and The Guess Who, letting my cat rub against my legs. The book ends with love and happiness, but in real life, love and happiness only precede pain. Later, after I learned how painful it is to truly crack, I stopped wanting my life to merit a heartbreaking Oprah book.

BLOCK, FRANCESCA LIA. *I WAS A TEENAGE FAIRY.* **NEW YORK: JOANNA COTLER BOOKS, 1998.**

I kept reading books from the Young Adult section of the library after I began slushing through poetry as a teenager, trying to be an adult reader, because Block's magic was still more appealing than the bonds of meter. I was allowed to fall in love with the girls and the boys in the books; I was allowed to want to leave rural New Jersey because "Los Angeles is a woman reclining billboard model with collagen-puffed lips and silicone-inflated breasts, a woman in a magenta convertible with heart-shaped sunglasses and cotton candy hair" (3). I wanted to be one of the beautiful, underweight, tragic girls in a Block novel. I read Block's books after my bipolar mood canyons were carved, but before I fell all the way into them, hit by jagged rocks on the way down. After leaving home, after I grew to legal maturity, I became what I always wanted to be: starved, mentally ill, tortured from the outside in and the inside out, city-dwelling, fast-driving. I never regretted asking for this. Reading the book again, after the rape, the diagnosis, the drugs, the other assault, I understood that this book glimmers not because of a delightful magic; it is more like psychosis.

WRIGHT, RICHARD. *NATIVE SON.* **1940. NEW YORK: HARPERCOLLINS, 1993.**

Sophomore year of high school, I was the teacher's pet. I worked on the literary magazine with Mr. Rowe, and he let me embroider during American Lit. After he assigned the part in which Bigger decapitates the woman's dead body in order to fit her into the furnace, Mr. Rowe made us write down what we remembered of the scene, down to the details. After that he tried to take me to the magazine's printer, a long car ride away, and I declined. At twenty-four, I still look sixteen, and when much older men find me captivating, I sometimes think of dismembered bodies.

WILLCOX, BRADLEY J., D. CRAIG WILLCOX, AND MAKOTO SUZUKI. *THE OKINAWA DIET PLAN: GET LEANER, LIVE LONGER, AND NEVER FEEL HUNGRY.* **NEW YORK: CLARKSON POTTER, 2004.**

All books change me, but diet and self-help books try to force the change to show. The results, success or failure, appear on the body. I adhered to the diet and lost a lot of weight my sophomore year of college. It probably wasn't the book that put me into starvation mode, but my misreading: I thought I needed to reduce my calories to seven hundred daily. My body was slight and perfect when I snared an acceptable boy; it was weak and starved when he pinned me down. I lent the book to a friend. I changed my diet like I changed my sheets.

ROBBINS, ALEXANDRA. *PLEDGED: THE SECRET LIFE OF SORORITIES.* **NEW YORK: HYPERION, 2004.**

I always sort of wanted to be a sorority girl. On campus, I would see girls walking in groups at night, dressed in gorgeously revealing black dresses and expensive heels. Their hair, light or dark, always appeared straight and shiny, and their spring indoor tans glowed. I knew I could pull it off: by senior year, I was completely lacking in sexual inhibition, I got drunk on weeknights, and I still maintained my lifetime 4.0 GPA. But even when I dip underweight, I still have stubborn love handles, which, according to Robbins, would be Sharpie-circled by my sisters in order to tell me why my body was defective. I began referring to the girls as "sorostitutes." I passed their houses every day when I walked to and from the Metro station, and I knew that there really was no secret life. Secrets were not the appeal. What I wanted was to be forced to perfect my body by something stronger than my internal drive. That, and access to frat boys. Sisterhood, I could take or leave.

SILKO, LESLIE MARMON. *CEREMONY.* **1977. NEW YORK: PENGUIN BOOKS, 1986.**

I can't blame my anthropology professor for getting excited about my enrollment in his North American Indians class. I was into it too. I wanted to learn all I could, and he was lonesome for the Indians, being too old to go play with the people in the Southwest who had fed him funny drugs and chuckled when he ran around at right angles. He told me he admired our ways. I didn't think he knew about my way of sleeping until noon, my way of keeping a pitcher of Kool-Aid spiked with Everclear in the fridge, or my way of crushing hard on my TAs and stalking their office hours, so I just thanked him for the compliment. I started every novel on his recommended reading list. The stories of days gone by might as well have been Shakespeare. For my final paper, I settled on *Ceremony* and ordered myself to become enamored: it was the newest book on the list, it was riddled with poems, and it was short. I read the first forty pages twice, and then caved and downloaded CliffsNotes. I felt like a bad Indian—this book was part of my canon. But I knew nothing about the horrors of war, dry places, witchcraft, or drinking from places of true torment. For my final paper, I skipped *Ceremony* and handed in a personal essay about being a suburban Indian. *I just don't get these books*, I thought, *they have nothing to do with me*, and I worked on carving out my spot in the literary world. For the last year of college, I let out war whoops, dressed in feathers, donned war paint so thick I forgot the color of my skin underneath. My copy of *Ceremony* has only one line highlighted from my attempt at engagement: "He's not full blood anyway" (33).

DANIELEWSKI, MARK Z. *HOUSE OF LEAVES*. 2ND ED. NEW YORK: PANTHEON, 2000.
I was jealous: Danielewski did whatever the hell he wanted. Different fonts and colors, sideways text, text in boxes, footnotes citing fake sources. My fiction was always Times New Roman, double-spaced, and the stories were always written in traditional narrative style, in which one paragraph flowed into the next, and the characters always changed or arrived or learned. I wrote a paper; I e-mailed his agent and publisher to ask how the manuscript arrived, and they said it looked the same then as it looked in my hands. It wasn't until I left college, began graduate study, and made academic choices of my own that I realized I could do whatever the hell I wanted, too.

FITZGERALD, F. SCOTT. *THE GREAT GATSBY*. 1925. NEW YORK: SCRIBNER, 1995.
I thought I wouldn't like it. I thought it was a dead white man book. In high school, I switched from honors English to stupid English to avoid reading it over the summer. But in college, when I realized I was going to be a writer, I let my teachers press the canon down into my brain. I began posing for photos for my future book jackets. I read *Gatsby* when I was beginning to lose my mind. I stood on a posh Northern Virginia balcony days after finishing the book, looking out at the "green breast of the new world" (189) that was the DC metro area. I knew that I had picked out my own green light; that my brain would never love me back; but I still believe that one fine morning—

FAULKNER, WILLIAM. *ABSALOM, ABSALOM!* **1936. NEW YORK: RANDOM HOUSE, 2002.**

I read this in college, sitting at the foot of my bed, in the four hours before my junior American Lit class started. When I got to class, I couldn't enter the discussion, because I couldn't remember the characters' names, or what the book was about, or anything that had happened in it. But I had read it for class, and as a writer, I was supposed to read Faulkner. That's the kind of thing writers do. If you asked me now, I'd probably say the book is about the South.

SHAKESPEARE, WILLIAM. *KING LEAR.*

I read five of his later plays junior year. The only lines I cared about, or even remember, are, "Use me well. / You shall have ransom. Let me have surgeons, / I am cut to th'brains," because I was.

ROTH, PHILIP. *AMERICAN PASTORAL.* **1997. NEW YORK: VINTAGE BOOKS, 1998.**

A girl from New Jersey commits an act of political terrorism; she becomes a murderer. The girl is raped twice; "The New Jersey girl rises to the level of psychosis" (261); couldn't the same be said about me? But I never killed anyone. I know my parents never thought, as Swede thought, "The worst of the world had taken his child. If only that beautifully chiseled body had never been born" (272). I am glad to have been born, glad to have suffered. I am glad that I can look back at my self-torment as though it happened to a fictional protagonist. I took the book to Starbucks, to random neglected lawns in front of the tinderboxes on Knox Road, to my favorite tunnel in all of Maryland, just so I could find a perfect place for repeatedly reading the same passages about rapes worse than mine—a life worse than mine. I started taking psych drugs and stopped reading the book; how sublime, droll, and disappointing real life is.

DICKENS, CHARLES. *HARD TIMES.*

I skimmed this, and used SparkNotes, and got the gist. I had read *A Tale of Two Cities*, so I could already say I had read Dickens. While reading *Hard Times*, I was busy titrating up to a therapeutic dose of Lamictal. The month-long titration period is notorious for its difficulty: for me, it brought on an acute bipolar mixed state. I don't remember why it was such a hard time for the characters, but I imagine it had something to do with being poor. I didn't have time to read because I was busy getting trashed every night, trying to date a guy who didn't treat me like a person, and sticking my butterfly knife into my arm at home after he hit on my friend in front of me at a bar. Sure, I wasn't poor—not even close—and I didn't work in a factory, but still, my experience was potent because I experienced it firsthand instead of through SparkNotes, and for this reason, senior year was a hard fucking time.

KING, STEPHEN. *CARRIE*. 1974. NEW YORK: SIGNET, 1975.

I adored Professor Satelmajer for putting this on the syllabus, because it was a bold move. By senior year, I was tired of reading high-quality literature and was glad to have something trashy to read. On my "books read.xls" spreadsheet, there is a month-long gap between my completion of this book for class and the completion of my next book for pleasure. Matching up that list with the list of my prescriptions filled at the University Health Center Pharmacy tells me that the gap coincided with my potentially-nearly-fatal reaction to Lamictal. I was bedridden for two weeks with a fever of 103, and then covered in a rash, and then immobilized by Benadryl, and then put on lithium instead of Lamictal. I thought my life was over; why read? To what end?

BENTLEY, TONI. *THE SURRENDER: AN EROTIC MEMOIR*. NEW YORK: REGAN BOOKS, 2004.

This is a woman who really loves anal. My best friend Stick had it on his shelf but had not read it; he just lent it out to his female friends. "Ass-fucking a woman is clearly about authority," Bentley writes. "The man's authority; the woman's complete acceptance of it" (91). I wondered whether she would love this surrender so much if it had been forced. When she wrote, "I want to die with him in my ass" (164). I decided that maybe she was right, maybe we do need to lose all power, and then maybe we regain it. The difference between us was that her loss was by choice. I will die with rape in my head, because it has never left my head. Stick mused that he and I would never be together because I wouldn't let him come on my face. Absolutely right.

PALAHNIUK, CHUCK. *FIGHT CLUB*. NEW YORK: HENRY HOLT & CO., 1996.

The summer after graduation, I read nothing. I drank soymilk-raspberry-flaxseed smoothies in the morning, tanned at the pool midday, worked in the afternoon, and went to bars in the evening. My doctor messed with my drugs because I was rapidly cycling through mania, depression, and mixed states. I kept hydrated. I spent myself silly. I was about to move across the country and set up a new life in Seattle. It had been years since I read *Fight Club*, but I still remembered Tyler's words:

> "If you lose your nerve before you hit the bottom," Tyler says, "you'll never really succeed."
>
> Only after disaster can we be resurrected.
>
> "It's only after you've lost everything," Tyler says, "that you're free to do anything." (70)

I lost all I could. I moved to Seattle, but I had a nice life, and I hadn't lost enough, so I still wasn't free. Then, under cloud cover, I lost my tan.

DIDION, JOAN. *RUN RIVER*. NEW YORK: POCKET, 1963.

Maybe the problem was that I don't care about what rich people do, but that's not really true, because I could read all day about Britney Spears and Paris Hilton. Maybe the rich people in *Run River* weren't fucked up enough. I probably could have gotten past page 86 (I don't even know how I got that far) if I hadn't been taking Abilify. A common side effect is akathisia: inner restlessness, chemical torture, inability to sleep past five in the morning, terror and doom, a compulsion to move. My heart felt like it had been dipped in lye. What did I care about old, rich people?

PROSE, FRANCINE. *BLUE ANGEL*. NEW YORK: HARPERCOLINS PUBLISHERS, 2000.

I read this in my secondhand pink armchair during the month between my move to Seattle and the start of school. The akathisia was unbearable, but I was going to make myself read a goddamn book after too many false starts, because reading books is something writers are supposed to do. I couldn't even read the new Roth. I picked up *Blue Angel* and took it slow: sentence to sentence, page to page. Then a chapter's finished, and I can go out for fresh air, or have some coffee, or go to the gym, or go to a thrift store, or do absolutely anything but sit in my pink armchair reading *Blue Angel*. I managed to finish. A week later, I went to my new doctor and got off the drug she said she would never prescribe to anyone.

WHITEHEAD, COLSON. *APEX HIDES THE HURT*. NEW YORK: ANCHOR, 2006.

I didn't like the book. But I could finally read again.

BOURKE, JOANNA. *RAPE: SEX, VIOLENCE, HISTORY.* **2006. NEW YORK: SHOEMAKER & HOARD, 2007.**

When we are raped, we want to read about rape, maybe to know that we aren't alone, or maybe to understand that it really did happen. We want to read about women who weren't drunk or drugged; who knew their attackers; who got away physically unscathed but emotionally etched for life; whose cleavage or bare legs or sultry eyes were asking for it; and who were still victims of crime, still didn't deserve it, still did what they had to do. Reading, in the end, didn't help, because published accounts are legitimate and real, and the one inside my head competes with psychosis.

HYMAN, MARK. *ULTRAMETABOLISM: THE SIMPLE PLAN FOR AUTOMATIC WEIGHT LOSS.* **NEW YORK: SCRIBNER, 2006.**

During the spring of my second year of grad school, I returned to the book that was once my anorexic bible. My wallet had just been stolen, and days later, I knocked a full mug of coffee into my laptop. I was making no money and finishing a graduate degree that would help me make even *more* no-money. I wanted the situation to get more desperate so I could finally hit bottom and then climb back out. Sometimes I think I'm stable, and sometimes I think I'm closer to the bottom than I realize. Hyman gave me some ideas. I would eliminate refined sugar. I would incorporate flaxseed and other sources of omega-3. I would minimize my exposure to toxins and eliminate factors that cause inflammation. My body would be mine again, underweight again, sleek again. I could not un-rape myself, but I could make myself wanted and flawless, could fix the body so that I could be certain that the body is not the problem here. One by one, even if I had to make myself an unrecognizable line drawing of my normal likeness, I would knock down every problem.

A Cascade Autobiography

PART 6

By the time I reached high school, being the only Indian around got lonesome, so I took what I knew from my books and my family and draped it in Indian-looking beads. Senior year, I only cut the bottom ten inches from my waist-long hair because it looked like something yanked from a drain, still black from a poor dye choice made to show my uniqueness when I embarked upon the great journey of high school, the ends marred by long splits. For years, I had kept that hair growing, as though it were an extension of my bloodstream and my Indian blood could increase as my ragged split ends grasped for my waist.

The Kindling Model in Bipolar Disorder

Every time people ask bipolar patients to take care of their own problems, the problems get worse. If a bipolar person goes untreated, she risks a worsening of the disorder. Episodes can increase in frequency and severity. Known as the kindling effect, this phenomenon was first observed in rats' brains that researchers stimulated using a low-dose electric jolt. Researchers then witnessed the effect in epileptics. They now apply it to bipolar patients who are asked to suffer through every cycle, use willpower and resolve, adopt a positive attitude, chin up, buck up, quiet down, stop crying on the subway, stop missing work, stop dragging everyone else down, start exercising, start meditating, did you ever try yoga?

Scientists apply the term "kindling" because the process is much like a log fire: by itself, the log is unsuitable for starting a fire, but the addition of smaller pieces of wood makes the fire easier to start. Allowing small episodes to smolder invites the brain to later burn.

In the sensitized brain, bipolar episodes begin to occur independent of stimulus. Episodes prime brain cells for repeated involvement, possibly leading to treatment-resistant bipolar disorder. A fire that has spread is harder to put out.

This model does not fully explain the disorder. Age, stress, and other factors, such as cocaine or alcohol abuse, contribute to increases in severity of episodes. Sometimes, though, you're fucked even if alcohol doesn't touch your lips until you're twenty years old, you never try cocaine, and you grow up with a perfect life and no stress at all. I will say right now that my childhood was as close to perfect as any can possibly be, with thickets and cats and forts and books and loving parents who raised me right and have always told me that I am brilliant and special, but still, my brain was askew, and no day ever felt completely right.

My eighth-grade guidance counselor suggested a bipolar diagnosis, but everyone else said it was teen angst, and so by age twenty-one I was writhing on the floor, wailing, or sitting in tunnels, or walking to nasty neighborhoods in the middle of the night.

Getting the brain right is the most important thing there is. Not the same as mind, the brain is a mass of tissue, another part of the body that can escape me, no different from a busted ankle or a nonfunctioning gallbladder. Since I became an adult, my

body has begun to fail. Forget the ankle. Those can be fixed for good if they get busted.
I want my brain.

The kindling process in my brain has stopped, or at least slowed, because of medication. I am free to focus on the other things that are still getting worse. My body is decaying as I let my brain marinate in trauma. Soon, maybe my whole body will be set aflame; just as researchers broadened the applicability of the kindling model to include bipolar disorder in addition to epilepsy, maybe they will expand the definition to cover overspending, overeating, promiscuity, and other kinds of escalation that rely on some fire in the head. A casual fuck or an ice cream cone here and there can sometimes accumulate, leading to bingeing. To nip bad behavior in the bud sounds quick and clean, as pleasant as a day with one's back to the sun, a gloved hand in garden soil, the other hand on a pair of shears, ready to cleanly slice huddled petals from stem. There is no metaphor that can explain the brain's openness to destruction. Fire, which has decimated forests and supported human life for more years than my brain can consider, comes pretty close.

A Cascade Autobiography

PART 7

I had heard that the best way to be a real Indian was to learn it from one's grandparents, but I hardly ever saw my Indian grandma. She lived thousands of miles away. My Irish grandma lived a couple hours away from me when I was a kid, until she and my grandpa moved to a retirement community just a few minutes from my house. Grandma Rosemary made me breakfast every Sunday after Mass, and from her, I have learned multitudes about being optimistic and kind. Grandpa John told me stories about the war, his close proximity to Eisenhower as flight engineer, and his travels around the world as a pilot. My dad told stories about Pennsylvania's coal region and fishing and mischief and the days of Catholic schools with inkwells and strict nuns. An avalanche of stories came to me, East Coast European-American ones, and the storytelling tradition was passed to me that way.

Prescribing Information

1/25/05 PLAN B DURAMED

Plan B is a backup plan that helps prevent pregnancy after some waste of sperm wastes his sperm in or around your vagina and you don't want to risk worrying whether you'll sprout an embryo with monster DNA that will claw at the inside of your womb and bleed you like a stuck pig. Plan B, however, will bleed you like a stuck pig. Plan B is not the abortion pill and it is not a substitute for routine birth control, which is why, although you may leave the gynecologist's office with a fistful of the barrier method, you will quickly realize the limitations of politely asking a college boy to slip on any sheath that might protect you from him.

2/18/05 ORTHO EVRA

Ortho Evra is a contraceptive patch used to prevent pregnancy when that boy who turned you from girl to gash keeps coming around with no condoms and no ears to hear about the stash you keep under the bed. Ortho Evra does not protect against HIV or other sexually transmitted diseases, but if you stop up your eggs, at least you will not have to carry his gremlin baby. Even if you do meet a suitable partner, do not let any boy draw on the Ortho Evra patch with a Sharpie.

8/28/06 ESCITALOPRAM OXALATE (LEXAPRO) 5 MG TABS

Lexapro is a prescription medicine used for the treatment of major depressive disorder. Depression is a real medical condition, the other name for the dread that pulls you down melting Maryland asphalt on steaming mornings while you drag your buttery bones along, wondering who liquefied your insides. Your condition requires diagnosis and treatment from a healthcare professional. When people suggest otherwise, you may experience urges to cut them in the face—speaking figuratively, that is. If you actually feel the urge to cut someone in the face, talk to your healthcare professional. He chose Lexapro for a reason, the reason being that he took a look at the numbers on the clinic entrance survey you filled out, he had no fucking clue what was wrong with you or what to put you on, and he started you on the drug he starts all his mentally interesting patients on. When your friends say, "Sweet, we fuckin' scored—yeah, of *course* you can snort that shit, you got it from, like, a shrink, right?," disregard their advice unless you want to feel like the skull-holes of your nose might burn clear through your flesh.

9/11/06 BUPROPION HCL SR (WELLBUTRIN) 100 MG

Wellbutrin may cause many side effects, including drowsiness, excitement, dizziness, and seizures, but the reason everyone gets so worked up about it is that it doesn't make the genitals limp. This, you won't care about at all: you'll be stunned by the drug's other point of appeal, the way your body fat seems to disappear one day. Your weight loss may fascinate you so intensely that you fail to notice the rapid cycling of your moods and your lack of sleep. Don't snort these pills—using this one recreationally might be possible, but you have a very limited supply. You'll probably like it a lot, feeling like you're on some legal version of coke, and it's a much cheaper habit. You won't identify this feeling as mania, because your diagnosis is depression, and Wellbutrin is used to treat depression, but nobody told you that a patient whose bipolar disorder slipped between the numbers on the clinic's mood scale survey should not take this drug on its own. You are now at risk for ripping your own heart out. You might flay your mind to pieces, and still, you might like the pain, but, after you lose a quarter of your body weight, half your friends, two-thirds of your dignity and all of your self-worth, when your doctor tells you it's time to go off it, you're not gonna have a choice.

10/9/06 LORAZEPAM (ATIVAN) 0.5 MG

Some long schooldays beg for high-potency chemical relaxation, and your fingers can stow loads of these Lilliputian pills under your tongue. As long as you don't imbibe, you can safely swallow more of these than you'd even be able to fit in your mouth. You show up for the anxiolytic effect, the evaporating panic, and you stay faithful for the hypnotic sleep, so the amnesic memory holes become the cost of calm. Ativan is highly addictive and you will quickly build up a tolerance. Careful: welcome this drug into your life and be prepared to wake up to see Ebay emails congratulating you on your purchases of such treasures as fake vintage Blondie posters and a genuine overpriced Farrah Fawcett poster—yes, the one with the nipple.

11/1/06 METHYLPHENIDATE (RITALIN) 5 MG

Methylphenidate belongs to the drug class called central nervous system stimulants. When a physician utters the word "methylphenidate" to a college-age patient, the drug has nearly synthesized in the young adult's body by the time "also known as Ritalin" crystallizes upon the eardrums. When your physician reaches for the green controlled substance pad, your stomach may squeal the way it used to at the sight of avocado flesh, now swooning for your new forbidden fruit. When your doctor tells you that it's only because of his concern for your lifetime four-point-oh transcript and your newfound inability to focus that he's affording you this opportunity for chemical brain-bending, you must not smile. Even if you nod soberly, he will know that you've done zanier things in your life—in your *month*—than put Ritalin up your nose. At least pretend that you won't copy a warning from a *Dateline* special because it seems like a good way to spend a Tuesday night. And when you do take that bottle home, swallow the drug as directed, and make every deadline your dog, try to save just one feeling in your gut as you model all your dresses and vacuum every inch of your kitchen. Say it so loud your clatter can't drown it out: "I practically can't get much higher than this."

While you wait to get your heart back, don't blame the drug. Ritalin is a federally controlled substance because it can be abused or lead to dependence. Keep Ritalin in a safe place to prevent misuse and abuse. Don't blame yourself too much, either. In ten minutes, this incident will amount to nothing more than a wasted pill and the memory of a brief fear that you may have killed your heart. But no matter your guilt, no matter your shame or wish for catharsis, don't ever tell your doctor what you did.

11/13/06 LAMOTRIGINE (LAMICTAL) 25 MG

Originally developed to treat epilepsy, Lamictal is now also part of the bipolar buffet, and you will be asked to add it to your plate when your doctor changes his mind about the whole depression thing. The pharmacist's warning will barely register, and you will not monitor your skin for rashes—after all, being medicated means being warned of death at every turn—and soon, you will come to rely on these little blue shield-shaped saviors, which grow in size as the milligrams increase, but first, you will be tested by a month-long period of terror in which your dosage will creep up toward 100 milligrams for fear of startling your immune system. Eventually, your mood will level out. Lamictal's mood-stabilizing properties will briefly offer to save your fucked-up life, but no sooner will your doctor declare you stabilized than he'll see you before him, howling, a speckled egg, abdomen exposed, your shadowed ribcage a spectacle, your blooming rash a once-in-a-career wonder. Your doctor will not look into the broken panes of your eyes as you ask him whether you're going to die. He will lean in close to look at the flush that had the potential to turn deadly but has been sapped of its danger, will say you caught it early enough to immobilize the reaction. You'll discontinue this drug that saved your mind, and you'll be just fine.

He will marvel at the marbling of your skin, cradling your wrist in his arm, his eyes macro-lens close to observe the rare bird of you, plumed in flannel pajama pants with dazzling sneakers poking out like showy tail feathers, and he will whisper, "I've never *seen* it before."

2/23/07 CETIRIZINE (ZYRTEC) 10 MG

Speckled like a nuclear-neon-pink piece of Easter candy on an exam room table, you may begin to pray to your fallen pills like false gods. Benadryl and Zyrtec will turn your skin back to lily petals, but without your psych drug of choice, you are a lost lamb. *Naked I came out of my mother's womb, and naked shall I return thither: the LAMICTAL gave, and the LAMICTAL hath taken away; blessed be the name of the LAMICTAL.* Take the pills that make you pale again. Forget you ever reacted.

2/23/07 LITHIUM CARBONATE 300 MG

Try not to let it get to you when your friends provide unsolicited medical advice to you based on the movie *Garden State*, in which Zach Braff's character can't *really* live until he ditches the lithium. Your doctor prescribed lithium for a reason: "I'm old school, lithium is old school, and this is the best idea I've got." Monthly blood tests should be scheduled to ensure that the dosage is safely docked in the therapeutic range. If you make your doctor explain this, he will tell you that lithium can easily reach toxic levels in the blood. You might not even ask, being more concerned with the inevitable weight gain. Even though lithium itself is little more than a bunch of fancy salts, it will turn you into a salt pillar when you hold old Lamictal bottles up to the light, looking back at your ruins. Put down the bottle. You're going to be just fine. Welcome to the world of fat.

6/28/07 ARIPIPRAZOLE (ABILIFY) 10 MG

When you insist on returning to your doctor to tell him that your head's still not on straight, do not be alarmed when he finally tells you he just doesn't know what to do this time. Do not be alarmed by the fact that he prescribes a drug from a group called "antipsychotics" despite the fact that the word sounds frightening. You can Google your drugs all you want, but by now, you should accept that understanding your brain is beyond you. You will have seen enough pill-bottle warning stickers that you're no longer alarmed by the potential threat of any side effect—*any* side effect, of *any* kind, *ever*, including death and weight gain—so you certainly won't be alarmed when your doctor says one of the side effects is feeling restless. When you see the drug ads, you will know why your doctor put you on Abilify: like many Americans, he saw the drug ad in which a woman pauses from her dog-walking to stand, one hand in her flowing hair and one on a leash, looking into verdant pastures and a road ahead, under the words "Are you ready to move forward?"

When you have three days' worth of the drug lubricating your synapses, you'll know why he shouldn't have put you on Abilify: because this "feeling of restlessness" is much closer to a feeling that your own body is attacking the idea of the rest of the world, its limits, and its stillness so hard that you are, pretty much, the one in the choke collar, the one on the leash.

7/12/07 CLONAZEPAM (KLONOPIN) 1 MG

Just tell him how long it's been since you've slept. You don't need to put on any show. Tell him the daylight is pooling in the backrooms of your eyeballs. He'll get out the controlled substance pad. Tell him about the internal organs you've been gluing into your scrapbook for safekeeping at dawn. Tell him about the dread, the leak that drips all night without sound. Just tell him what you need.

09/24/07 QUETIAPINE FUMARATE (SEROQUEL) 100 MG OR TABS

Some people try one, two, handfuls of psych meds before giving up and settling for crazy. Others stick with the game awhile until they find the one they're going to be with for a long time. When you find Seroquel, it will be as though you are finding a husband, and you say your vows. Yes, Seroquel may cause unprecedented weight gain— you might find a photo online of a man's massive gut tattooed with the drug name in some unfortunate font. You may experience a constant, overwhelming desire to get shitfaced on weeknights. But the drug will knock you out in ten minutes, and even better, you may experience feelings that you are that woman in that drug advertisement field, looking at a long road and a far-off future.

You'll always be bipolar. You'll never stop gaining weight and you'll probably die of liver failure if you don't stop your drinking. No drug is going to make you stop being the person that you are. But stay faithful to Seroquel. You'll never again need to cheat with a friend's Ambien on a thousand-mile night, and you may put to rest the deep fear lodged like an old bullet in your gut, the nagging worry that there will be a day you lose yourself completely, lose all ability to keep your shit together, start wandering the streets of Seattle, where you might make dukes and duchesses of all the people wearing fresh kicks, and distribute your possessions equally among them, eventually wander onto I-5 naked, and neglect to remove your puffy body from the path of the gleaming Lexus SUV of a recent college grad with a newly minted degree in something glossy, whose cheek melts into her iPhone while her eyes admire her eyes in the rearview mirror, unsure of whether she's really achieved natural-looking makeup, or whether it's obvious that she's trying to look fresh-faced, but either way, her gas tank is full and ready for that big road ahead, the one that you used to think was so impossibly long.

But no—you have your cocktail settled. You will not go crazy. Taking your Seroquel, Lexapro and lithium as prescribed each day will let you drive with a clean windshield. You will know they're working because you'll nearly forget that all of this ever happened. Every morning and night, you are given a choice: you can live in this world, your brain doused in more chemicals than the fruits on the produce pesticide watch list in your wallet, or you can go organic and wild, as you were created. This is no choice between the blue pill and the red, blissful ignorance or a chance to live real. How many sides to the pill that fits perfectly into your heart and turns in your lock? Every day, you will recommit yourself to the capsule and the tablet, the pink pill and the white, the yellow, because you will want to live among the people of this world.

You will experience the unpleasant side effect known as the acquaintance's innocent question: "Don't you ever think about not taking those nasty chemicals?" and you will feel your slick tongue in your mouth, anchored to bone, writhing like a sea anemone. The muscles will pulse and want to tell the things that aren't said in polite company, the truth about how to keep a bipolar person from turning feral, or worse. But your tired, billowy lungs just sigh out an answer: "You know, I've never thought about that."

A Cascade Autobiography

PART 8

In college, I tried telling stories that weren't mine. I showed up pale and brilliantly bare-limbed to my honors dorm toward the end of a hot Mid-Atlantic summer, and when word got out about my scholarship, kids said, haven't the Indians already mooched off this country enough with their casino-building and slipping loose from tax-paying? I burrowed into the library and made scattershot efforts to learn what I could about Indian things—languages, histories, stories—and created my own fictions from them, hoping to prove myself that way, if I carried no proof within me.

I thought I was a full half-Native and a full half-Ukrainian until I was about ten. The simple question of "How much?," the wish to split someone's ancestry into neat compartments, can actually tear a person limb from limb. I wouldn't know it until reaching graduate school, but the tendency to divide Indian ancestry into numerical parts is far from natural—it has been written into American law since the colonial period. Now, as a condition of enrollment, many tribes require individuals to demonstrate a minimum degree of ancestry, known as "blood quantum." Once I figured that out, it took me even longer to understand that blood quantum has nothing to do with blood—there is no such thing as Indian albumin, Irish hemoglobin, Ukrainian leukocytes, or French platelets. The veins and arteries do not split in those who are mixed, and the blood does not contain the oily and watery liquids of disparate ethnicities. "Blood" is just a metaphor, and it's not much of one. Looking beyond the fractional diminishing from generation to generation, I began to wonder whether the

blood does contain something real, an essence that cannot
be neatly halved.

Dear Diary

12/22/06, 12:25 p.m.

I think I am going to keep a Dear Diary because I like to write things down. Private
things. I can't tell anyone what's in my head. It's getting claustrophobic. A balloon I
have to let air out of slowly. Deflate my disorder. So here is my new Word doc diary.
It's Christmas Break, I am bored at parents' house, sick of working on senior project,
and I have a lot to say, and here is something I can't say to my parents, even though I
thought they wanted me to be skinny, because everyone in the world thinks everyone
else should be skinny, because that's just how the world works. This is how I got skinny:

I think the food other people eat is disgusting.

White bread is disgusting. (I am seriously getting so grossed out thinking about it.)

Pork, ham, and beef are disgusting.

Most cheese is disgusting.

Milk is disgusting.

Butter is disgusting.

White bread is still disgusting.

Jelly is disgusting. (Preserves are not.)

Italian ice is disgusting.

Apple pie is disgusting.

Fatty fish is disgusting.

Vodka is disgusting. (Whiskey is not.)

Raw fish is disgusting.

I guess chicken is also disgusting.

Sugar is disgusting.

PIZZA IS SO DISGUSTING>OMG

Everything but fruit and nuts is disgusting, basically. Fruit and nuts and whiskey.
Protein powder.

. . . and prescription drugs.

Wellbutrin is my favorite food. Wellbutrin made me skinny. If I hadn't gone crazy last summer, I'd still be a cow.

12/25/06, 1:55 a.m.

(I've done things the bipolar book talks about. You have to say you're sorry for what you did when you weren't you. You have to say sorry for the two months when you wouldn't leave the house without high heels on, and somehow, your feet never hurt, and you didn't need to sleep, and you ran two miles a day, and you never saw your parents, and you got a full-body sunburn, and and and and—)

Tomorrow, a Christmas dinner I won't eat. I could tell my parents were horrified tonight when I didn't eat spaghetti for dinner with them and just had a smoothie and a few pieces of the wheat bread my mom made. She was also horrified later when I pitched a fit over the fact that she used half white flour, and I don't eat white flour. They think I am anorexic. I am not anorexic. I'm just a health nut now that I'm pumping my body full of chemicals and beer, so I can balance the toxin load. They used to think I looked good. They changed their minds. I'm just trying to be good.

12/26/06, 5:20 p.m.

Dad and I keep disagreeing over organic food.

Today it started when Mom and I went to ShopRite. The store brand canned vegetables and beans are all organic now. There's no ShopRite brand vegetables without "Organic" printed on the label. Okay.

I got some corn and beans and Mom said, "I don't want organic."

I said, "There's nothing but organic if you want the cheapest brand." She didn't get it. I explained it again at home.

Then Dad: "I don't see how they can call it 'organic,' that's stupid, it's corn, of course it's organic. It's made of organic molecules and . . . " (Blah, blah, blah, biologist talk.)

Elissa: "Exactly. Corn is organic. That is the point of labeling it as organic."

Dad: "Why bother?"

Elissa: "THEY COULD PUT THINGS OTHER THAN CORN IN THE CAN. THERE COULD BE CHEMICALS ON THE CORN. PESTICIDES AND SHIT. BUT THERE AREN'T. IT MEANS THERE IS ONLY REGULAR REAL CORN IN THE CAN. THERE IS CORN. AND SALT. AND WATER."

Dad: "But all plants are made of organic matter and . . . " (So on and so on and—)

Elissa: "YEAH, BUT—" (And then we eventually stop talking about it.)

Okay, so, it's true that I don't know what organic actually means, but the book I read says EAT ORGANIC and I truly believe if I do, I will live forever, like a better version of Gwyneth Paltrow, clean-bodied and thin, and I don't like the thought of toxic sludge coating all my cells.

12/27/06, 11:00 a.m.

Every night now I dream about boys.

I'm looking at pictures of Nikes like some people look at porn. I just saw a purple suede pair of Jordan 5s. (There is no shoe like a Jordan 5! That is what I have and they sell for way too much on this site I'm at.)

I like myself better when there's less of me. By percentage I am more sneaker than girl.

12/28/06, 9:51 p.m.

I got my teeth out today. It was a mad weird experience. I took three Ativan in the car so I'd chill out, which would make it easier for Dr. K., and so I might be able to forget the whole thing happened. I knew it wasn't going to be so bad because he's done it before, on the other side of my mouth. Just yanked out the teeth, no surgery, just Novocain. The man is a fucking professional.

I didn't even realize the needle was going in until after it was in. I didn't give a fuck. Then when my face was all numb he took the teeth out. He showed me that they had rings on them, like the rings on a tree—they show that my mom took antibiotics or something during her pregnancy. He said it didn't mean anything, it was just a thing that happens. That was pretty cool.

Then Mom and I went to the indoor farmers' market and bought stuff. I got strawberries, kiwis, bread, and soy milk. Mom took care of me. I am glad I didn't have to interact with people, because when I got to the car, I realized the inside of my mouth was covered in blood. Blood all over my teeth. Like I'd been in a fight. When I got home, I slept for seven hours. I woke up with blood dripping out of my mouth onto the pillow, so I put some more gauze in and a towel on the pillow. It's still bleeding now.

I don't know anyone else who gets their wisdom teeth out this way, no anesthesia, no painkillers, just Novocain. Sometimes I take a break from hating myself and think I might be pretty fuckin' BALLERRRR.

CATCHER IN THE RYE reading notes: Ch. 7 is good to look at for access, dispensation of information, withholding. Talks about what's wrong when that's not really what's wrong.

Keeps describing setting as depressing.

12/29/06, 7:50 p.m.

I am terrified of the rest of my life. I am nearly in tears over insurance. It's easy now—it's dad's, it's good, it's reliable. After I turn twenty-three, I'm on my own. My med bills would total maybe $400 per month without insurance, so if I don't get a teaching assistantship in grad school, I'm shit outta luck. I hate that my school choice might come down to this. If I go off Lamictal, I am seriously going to eventually kill myself. I'm not suicidal but I will be if I stay bipolar, untreated, for any length of time. Not fair that my sanity might end up being all about the benjamin$.

12/30/06, 3:19 p.m.

Glaxo Smith Klein drug site: "Remember, bipolar disorder is usually a lifelong condition. Your healthcare provider may have prescribed LAMICTAL to help you achieve your long-term treatment goals." Thanks GSK. Please make me a drug that won't require me to start hooking if I want to afford it. Then I can think about the long term. I keep fucking with my Excel budget spreadsheet but I can't make the numbers work without health insurance. (I think my mouth is bleeding again cause I keep fucking with that too.)

1/1/07, 2:21 a.m.

From the CrazyMeds discussion board:

Quote from waxleaves (that's me) **on 31 Dec. 2006 at 17:08:**

I've been on Lamictal for a couple months now, it's working great, I have no intention to stop, but people (GP, family, friends) have been telling me that I should stop at some point "just to see." No, I shouldn't, right? I'd risk having it not work when I'd need to start up again?

Reply: I think these people might be confused about what condition you are taking medication for. Bipolar disorder is a lifer's thing. It doesn't go away. People generally stay on meds for life. If you found one that works, then don't run the risk of messing it up the second time round—and if you go off your meds, and you are BP, the chances are *extremely extremely* high there will be a second, third, fourth time round. Your family (and unfortunately your GP too, it seems) seems to think that you have a condition such as situational depression that can resolve itself and go away, never to return. That simply is not how this beast works. They need to learn more. Basically how meds and BP work is when you find one that works, you hold on tight and keep it for as long as it works. Stopping "just to see" is a fool's game when you're bipolar (it doesn't matter what medication we're talking about).

For life. It doesn't go away. People generally stay on meds for life. When you find one that works, you hold on tight and keep it for as long as it works.

WHEN YOU FIND ONE THAT WORKS, YOU HOLD ON TIGHT AND KEEP IT FOR AS LONG AS IT WORKS.

Unless you get that rash they're talking about. OK, I have a secret: Lamictal is working so well that if I get a rash on it, I am not going to tell the doctor. Wait it out and hope it's from some rogue fabric softener or some shit. Because if they take me off it I'll be sick again.

Oh, Happy New Year. My New Year's = eating a whole box of ice cream sandwiches with my family, watching the ball drop on NBC, and then immediately, seconds into 2007, I start feeling the dread.

1/1/07, 9:13 p.m.

Noah (9:00:03 PM): hahaha ok sorry to break the conversation flow but you have to hear this. my raisin bread bag says *"The government demands that there be a minimum amount of raisins in each loaf of raisin bread. But this is not good enough for Sun-Maid. Our bread has 50% more raisins than the government asks for."*

1/1/07, 9:26 p.m.

I eat 100% whole wheat bread. Preferably with flaxseed, for omega-3 fatty acids. This is because this kind of bread has nutritional value. I only eat things with nutritional value, unless SOMEONE gives me LARGE QUANTITIES OF CHOCOLATE for Christmas (Mom). 100% whole grain bread has many vitamins and nutrients. It has a lot of fiber. It does not make me fat, eating this way, because this is real food. One slice is filling. Trust me. I lost twenty-three pounds in 2006, the doctor's records show! Only eight more to go before I'm underweight, then two more and I'll be at the weight I was before I started gaining (113 freshman year of high school). It WILL happen. Mark my fucking words.

So I read somewhere that if you can squish the bread in your hands, the way you can squish a loaf of Wonder Bread, that bread will go straight to your gut-fat.

Anyway, I was looking for 100% whole wheat but of course out here in the boonies you can't get health food. I've put on a pound during this ten-day period at home. In the ShopRite, ALL the bread in the store that says wheat on the package basically appears to be white bread. So it has the appearance of health, but still tastes like white bread.

THEN IT'S WHITE BREAD
IT'S FUCKING WHITE BREAD
IT'S NOT ANY HEALTHIER

IT'S PROBABLY WHITE BREAD DYED BROWN

1/2/07, 12:11 a.m.
Last year I did the "I resolve to lose thirty pounds" thing, but if I do that again this year, I'll die. Wellbutrin is my favorite food.

1/3/07, 1:02 p.m.
Are those my ribs? I thought that was fat. That used to be fat. That's not fat. I do have a very large ribcage. Do I have a problem? Should I be talking to someone? Am I unattractively skinny? I have never been skinny in my life. When I was in eighth grade I was skinny but gangly and awkward. People used to *say* I was skinny and not mean it, but now they actually mean it. I know because their voices sound different when they say it.

Also, I'm a size zero.

Also, none of my old clothes fit. At all. I have to decide whether to get new bikini bottoms because even my boardshorts are too big. Hey, why not? Now that I'm back in College Park, I should go to Bikini Splash today. I bet I'll look good! For the first time!

1/4/07, 8:30 p.m.

My Levis are really baggy. That's not fucking good because they are a size zero. And last night Stacey took this photo of me:

[Photo of me grinning with hair heavily gelled into a fauxhawk, hoop earrings, neck tendons standing out.]

And I said, "Holy fuck, is that what I look like?"

Because I look fucking emaciated there.

I have a Celine Dion neck.

In the mirror I still look fairly chunky.

I think I have a problem.

But there's no way in hell I'm gonna let myself put on any weight.

1/6/07, 4:30 p.m.

I mean . . . I don't know . . . I think things are going well.

Some special things that I know are cool about me and other people know are cool, too:

I have five pairs of high-tops

I once hacked into the email account of Nirvana's bassist

I love mid- to late-90s mainstream hip hop

And new wave

And cock rock

I am batshit crazy

I have pink patent leather high heels

I fence

I scream when I fence

I have been to a nude beach

Nude

I Work For The Government

I eat very little high-fructose corn syrup

Or processed starches

And so I lost 25 pounds

I have a naval officer's hat and yes, it's a good story

I've yelled at someone who had just pulled a knife on me and then I told him to get the fuck out of my life

Whatever, I'm happy, or at least not unhappy about the stuff that was bothering me.

But it could just be mania.

P.S. Yesterday I hung out with Pete and he hit-and-ran, but didn't run too far, and parked his car in the lot next to where it happened, and then we had ice cream and nothing happened. It's good to be back in College Park.

1/16/07, 6:39 p.m.

I don't know anything about anything. I think I'm happy and then it's all fake. Mania isn't happiness.

Also, my life is so stupid I just made my therapist cry when I was talking about stuff. I was talking about the old rape or something and she starts tearing up and then crying and I was like, "Why are you crying?" and she said, "Your life," and I said, "Is it really that bad?" Because I thought this was just growing up. Maybe not. Maybe I'm special in the worst way.

2/24/07, 11:19 a.m.

Things were going really, really well for a while, but today I'm the most heartbroken I have been in a long, long time.

My medication dosage was finally perfect, and I was finally in a good place—happy, clear, motivated. Finally, after probably a couple dozen appointments with my psychiatrist, we were going to slowly stop seeing each other. Then, a few days after our last talk, I got this rash. ALL OVER MY BODY. Lamictal has this infamous rash—if you get it, you could be dead in a week if you don't stop your meds. It's this drug reaction, Stevens-Johnson Syndrome. It was probably that.

See, I've been sick for almost three weeks. I started out with a fever of 103. The fever went down quickly, but I've been congested and tired still, so I went to the health center, and the doctor noticed that I had a rash on my torso. While I was in the health center, it spread to most of my body. They gave me a shot of Benadryl. They also sent me upstairs to talk to my psychiatrist and he told me I had to stop taking Lamictal immediately. I cried in his office.

He said in all his years as a psychiatrist, he's never seen The Rash. It's like legend. He said, "Why did this have to happen to one of my favorite people?"

I'm off Lamictal. I'm on Lithium. This is a bitch for so many reasons.

Lamictal was the only thing that helped me get it together after I crashed as low as I did. It picked me up out of the scariest time in my life, when the inside of my head was the most terrifying place I'd ever been, except I was there all the time for months, and I could feel myself not present as a person anymore. I didn't think I was ever coming back. Then I did. Now, I don't know what will happen.

And I still don't know if I have this syndrome and what it means for me. Like, did I have a deadly condition? Will I ever be able to go back on? Am I out of the woods, or is something bad happening inside? It's pretty clear that I did have it, but you can't know for sure without a biopsy, and I didn't have one.

And also, I've been wearing this medical ID bracelet for a while saying what I'm on in case anything happens to me and whoever is taking care of me needs to know I'm taking Lamictal, because if you immediately stop taking it you can have a grand mal seizure. Bad shit can happen. So I stopped taking it and I don't know what's going to happen. Like if I'll have a seizure.

And Lithium is scary.

I can't talk to anybody about this. I'm crazy. I can't talk to anybody about how I'm crazy. I think Stick knows I'm really torn up inside and is going to keep me company and let me talk this evening.

I feel so mortal. I'm tired of this body. For the past couple of years it's been a bitch to me. First my gallbladder died, then my liver wouldn't take over for it. My brain is misshapen and its chemicals are off. My body can't work with what I put in it.

Oh, and after I almost died, Susan the iPod DJ called me up and nearly talked me into running to the liquor store for her so she could have wine with her pasta dinner with her also-under-twenty-one girlfriend, and yes, I did tell her that I almost died, and no, she didn't care.

I only write in this when something sucks.

3/16/07, 7:17 p.m.

I went to the doctor today and it is back to the drawing board. Lithium is obviously not the drug for me. I thought he was going to up my dose since it hasn't been working, but he said that for bipolar depression (as opposed to mania), the drug works better at lower doses. So the Wellbutrin is going back up. Hopefully that'll help me lose those five pounds I put on, and if nothing else, it'll send me into a hypomania that will help me get my thesis done.

I said, "I wish I hadn't gotten that rash." Which is an understatement. He said he had been thinking the same thing in the car this morning because he knew he was going to see me today. He had never seen anyone get The Rash before. It sounds like I am a unique patient. Also, one day I came in absolutely miserable, and it was a bad scene, so he upped the Lamictal and lowered the Wellbutrin, and he said that was the first time in sixteen years that he fucked with two drugs at the same time.

I'm kind of blue. I'm going to lie down. When I wake up I am going to eat a cookie some rabbi gave me.

3/22/07, 9:35 p.m.

Here was my day, courtesy of pills.

1. I got out of bed way late because I had knocked myself out with Ativan last night. People had been over and I was still anxious because people make me anxious.

2. I see the bottle of Ritalin next to the computer and I think I might have taken two of them and that is how I finished a full draft of my thesis today.

3. I am on Lithium so I can't remember whether I took Ritalin or not.

4. I lost 2 pounds and went down from 27% to 25% body fat since I upped the Wellbutrin last week, according to my scale, of which I am suspicious. Once again, eating is a chore, which kind of sucks, but fortunately, I'm back to only wanting very healthy food.

5. I miss Lamictal so bad it hurts. That rash was a fucking curse. I must have had bad karma. Well, maybe my karma is really good now, because I have gone through a period of suffering. I think my doctor has a plan in case my current drugs don't kick in, and I fear that, because those drugs would make me fat, I would have to buy new pants/ hate myself.

3/24/07, 7:01 p.m.

Colin (6:04:01 PM): dude

Colin (6:04:07 PM): my washing machine is on fire

Elissa (6:04:31 PM): WHAT

Elissa (6:24:55 PM): did you put out the fire / decide what bar we're going to

5/22/07, 2:35 p.m.

Yesterday I graduated. A useless degree, headed for another. I cried twice at graduation. Once when my ex's name was called—he's only a year behind schedule, in the end—and once when Colin's name was called—I don't know how he did it. I had a bunch of cords and tassels and shit on. Summa cum laude. Phi Beta Kappa. English Honors. University Honors. Thesis completed under the direction of Maud Casey. English Excellence. Creative Writing Award. It was like, for one day I had a reminder that I've still got my brain. Today all those weird words stopped meaning anything.

Last night Stephany said, "I heard about all the honor cords you had on at graduation. None of us knew you were smart."

5/22/07, 9:59 p.m.

Last night Stacey and I were walking from Commons to the parking garage to go to the liquor store when we spotted this big-ass praying mantis. We took a picture. I think the flash stunned it a little. It looked really scared. I had never seen one before. I said, "I think that shit is endangered." Stacey said, "I wanna put out my cigarette on it."

A Cascade Autobiography

PART 9

I learned in science class that some genetic material is passed down through mitochondrial DNA, which live in women's eggs. This was the limit of my understanding. Instead of researching this nugget's veracity, I chose to seize upon it, believing it meant that my core had been formed by elements handed down from woman to woman through the generations like a scepter. I reasoned that something in me, holding court in every cell, was truly indigenous.

How that hidden code manifested in my outward form, though, was hard to say. In summer, my skin tanned easily. I would admire the contrast between my fingers and the white flesh between them, because by December, I'd be even paler than many of the Euro-American kids at school, especially the ones whose families had come over from Italy a few generations back. The only Indians I'd ever seen were the ones I was related to, the ones in the movies, and the ones who danced at the powwows held every summer of my childhood on the grounds of a winery ten minutes away from my house. My mother, brother, and I would spend all year being the only Indians around, as far as we knew. In July, Indians from all over would converge at the local powwow, bringing with them beads and feathers, suede and abalone, weave and fringe. I wondered what they had been born with that I hadn't, since we were all Indian yet they had these steps in them, these rhythms, these fur wraps and plumes that made them seem part bird or part otter. I wondered whether I would grow up to be Indian like that. I thought I might be part animal, too—part guinea pig, hamster, crawfish, cat, all my pets, as we got along so well when we played, and they understood me better than any classmate. Still, before I was old enough to know what "Indian" meant, I knew we were produced in at least two varieties. I was unlike the powwow people who came from elsewhere. I asked my mother where I could learn to dance like that and she said she didn't know.

Fucker and Fucked

**WE HOOKED UP OR WHATEVER: A RECENT DEVELOPMENT IN THE
LANGUAGE OF SEX**

"When one man fucks many women he is a playboy and gains status; when a woman is fucked by many men she degrades herself and loses stature," wrote Robert Baker in 1971.[2] Thirty-five years later, in the social sphere of undergraduates at the large and liberal University of Maryland, the notion hardly seems true.[3] While some students are hesitant to engage in sexual acts with many (or any) partners, others do so with boyfriends, girlfriends, friends, acquaintances, and strangers. In this casual sexual climate, in which sex is the pinnacle of sexual contact but by no means the only activity in which students regularly engage, "hooking up" is a normal and socially acceptable form of interaction. The term *hook up* is difficult to define because in using it, the speaker aims to avoid specifying an act or set of acts, and because it can also serve as a catch-all term. The use of *hook up* is much less prevalent than terms that specifically refer to the act of intercourse, such as *have sex, fuck, sleep with*, and *do*,[4] but its applicability differs in that it encompasses acts other than penetration as well.

I conducted interviews with ten undergraduates, five male and five female,[5] from the University of Maryland, between the ages of nineteen and twenty-three, with the intent to determine how they use the term *hook up*. I found that *hook up* was used in rare and particular instances, and that the other terms used to refer to sexual acts were noteworthy as well: a speaker's choice to use a particular term has a dramatic effect on the characterization of a situation and reflects the speaker's attitude toward sex. Symmetrical expressions such as *hook up, have sex, sleep with* and *do it* function differently than do *fuck* and expressions of things done to, rather than with, a partner. However, I do not find, as Baker does, that this asymmetry is based in gender and conceptions of anatomy as much as it is based in which party has more control, power, and agency in

---

2   Robert Baker, "'Pricks' and 'Chicks': A Plea For 'Persons,'" 179.

3   Academic language must be confident, more confident than my voice tended to be when I insisted that I was not a slut. So, knowing that I was never truly a playgirl, I had to open with lies.

4   Bang, slam, nail, screw, hump, enjoy. Get laid, have at it, hit it, score. Bone. Ball. Make love? Fuck no.

5   I had fucked three of the interviewees.

the situation. *Hook up* is a fitting term, because of its vagueness and broad applicability, for indicating that a sex act has taken place without assigning agency to either party.[6]

BACKGROUND

In his 1971 article "'Pricks' and 'Chicks': A Plea for 'Persons,'" Robert Baker lays out the concept of asymmetry in the grammar of discussing sex:

> Thus, we would not say "Jane did it to Dick," although we would say "Dick did it to Jane." Again, Dick bangs Jane, Jane does not bang Dick; Dick humps Jane, Jane does not hump Dick. In contrast, verbs like "did it with" do not require an active role for the male; thus, "Dick did it with Jane and Jane with Dick." Again, Jane may make love to Dick, just as Dick makes love to Jane.[7]

Baker argues that through looking at the language, we can see that people conceive of the male role as active and the female role as passive, and he rejects the notion that these roles are based in the man's anatomically granted ability to insert and the resulting role of the woman as receptacle.

Janice Moulton also takes up the issue of grammatical symmetry in her 1975 article "Sex and Reference." She focuses not only on insertion but also on orgasm and argues that the act of intercourse, even when described using symmetrical terms, is off-balance:

> [S]exual intercourse formally begins when the primary focus for sexual stimulation in the male (the penis) is inserted into a container particularly well suited to bring about the male orgasm (the vaginal orifice). Although the dictionary merely says that sexual intercourse "involves" this insertion, anything prior to this inser-

---

6 Although an analysis of college students' idle chatter about their sexual proclivities might seem like a waste of academic energy, as Sally McConnell-Ginet writes in "The Sexual (Re)Production of Meaning: a Discourse-Based Theory," "Language matters so much precisely because so little matter is attached to it: meanings are not given but must be produced and reproduced, negotiated in situated contexts of communication" (209). This paper seeks to explore not only what some might consider the lowest form of trash language of the young adults currently navigating our academic system, but to explore the power dynamics conveyed by the word choice. Personally, being unlike most young people, I always refused to say "hook up." If I fucked him, that's what I would say, that I fucked him. If he came on my belly before we could fuck, that's what I'd say. My speech would be more precise than any man's hands. If we kissed and he decided he had to go, and never called me, my mouth would be too busy licking wounds to speak any words about it at all.

7 Baker, 174-5.

tion is termed "foreplay" or "preliminaries"; the real thing does not
begin until the insertion occurs.[8]

This argument is useful in considering the separation of *hooking up* and *having sex*;
although foreplay is a different notion and was not discussed in any of the interviews
I performed,[9] there existed a definite sense of sex as the end of the sexual spectrum
opposite kissing, and of all other acts as precursors to sex. Moulton also notes the connection between asymmetry and vulgarity, specifically discussing *fuck* and pointing
out, "If he fucked her, it does not follow that she has fucked him, but only that she has
been fucked by him. The grammar of the word 'fuck' does not imply that he and she
are equally involved in the activity."[10]

In a 2000 study, Sarah K. Murnen finds that among the college men and women
she studied, "men were more likely than women to report using degrading terms to refer to male genitals and female genitals and were more likely to report using aggressive
terms to refer to copulation";[11] she concludes that "[t]he data generally supported the
idea that language reflects a conception of male sexual power over females."[12] However,
determining what is "degrading" is problematic because much of the slang college students typically use to refer to sex and genitals could be thought of as degrading, and a
person who chooses to use this type of slang may have to use those colloquial terms if
she wishes to avoid speaking in more technical, less conversational language.[13]

THE STUDY

The purpose of my study was to determine the patterns of usage of *hook up*. I hypothesized that participants would use the term to convey that sexual activity took place
without providing details in order to maintain privacy, to speak about sexual activity

---

8 Janice Moulton, "Sex and Reference" (1975), 186.

9 In college culture, foreplay did not matter. Penetration mattered. His flourishing finish mattered.
His leaving satisfied mattered. Everything else was a nicety, formality, or necessity in order to get him
hard. Female arousal was not necessary for intercourse if a little Astroglide was kept under the bed
or in the purse.

10 Ibid., 185.

11 Sarah K. Murnen, "Gender and the Use of Sexually Degrading Language," *Psychology of Women
Quarterly*, 24 (2000), 320.

12 Ibid., 323.

13 I used the word *cunt* frequently and defiantly, feeling that some men said *cunt* like they owned
the word. But "vagina" sounded to me like a thing that was falling out of the body in pieces, onto a
metal table in a gynecologist's office. It was nothing as cute as a cooter, pussy, coochie, muff, or beaver,
nothing as grotesque as an axe wound, cock holster, or pair of beef curtains (yes, I did hear those
terms in use). Mine was, for a while, a cunt, because a cunt sounded like it should bear fangs.

not limited to intercourse, and to express that some sexual act unknown to the speaker had taken place. In order to collect data, I conducted ten recorded interviews with University of Maryland undergraduates between the ages of nineteen and twenty-two, split evenly by gender. Two participants (one male and one female) identified themselves as bisexual, two (one male and one female) identified themselves as homosexual, and six identified themselves as heterosexual.

All participants are friends with whom I had previously held intimate conversations about sex and romance.[14] I attempted to choose a group of interviewees that reflected a variety of social circles to ensure that my study would not be limited to a narrow subgroup of university students and that the range of sexual experience among participants would be broad as well.

Participants were asked to respond to a series of questions about sexual practices, their own and their friends', and about how they and their friends customarily talked about sex. They were encouraged to tell interesting stories they had heard and to talk about sexual acts other than intercourse. The questions were developed with an aim to encourage interviewees to talk about sex without feeling that they had to expose themselves in a way that made them uncomfortable, yet the questions were open-ended enough that interviewees could share more information about themselves if they wished to.

THE PARTICIPANTS

Male #1, who will hereinafter be referred to as "Jacob,"[15] speaks generally and often vaguely about the sexual experiences he has had, has not had, and would like to have. He is sexually experienced but has not had sex in quite some time.[16] However, he talks about sex often. He speaks about sex symmetrically, partly because his general and removed language strips the people involved or potentially involved of most of their agency. Sex, to him, is something that he experiences, and that happens to him, more than something he does.

---

14   And, recall, I'd fucked three of them.

15   I tried for years to fuck this interviewee. He wouldn't have it. Then we came to love each other like blood relatives. Like I was his mother, grabbing his arm when his drunk ass thought it'd be funny to grab a cop's butt. I'm sure that at one time he really was sexually desirable to me.

16   It made me crazy. I didn't want to have sex with him anymore, by the time I interviewed him, but I remembered needing to have sex with him at one point in the past, and knowing that he hadn't actually been fucking and seemed to sort of want to have been fucking and knowing that he knew I wanted to fuck him, all made me somewhat upset, so during the interview, I drank a lot of rum.

Male #2, or "Kyle,"[17] has a great deal of sexual experience with both men and women and is currently in a committed relationship. There are definite actors in the sexual acts he talks about. It often cannot be assumed that he is talking about intercourse, and the active party may be male or female. Although asymmetry appears in individual references to acts, he displays no general or gender-based asymmetry in attitude. Although he seems to consider one person to usually have a more active role in the sexual act, he does not delineate roles by gender. In addition, he seems to note a difference between doing *with* and doing *to*.

Male #3, or "Theo,"[18] has no (or very little) sexual experience. There is little variety in his terminology: *have sex* is his preferred term when referring to the act itself, but he also sometimes says *do it* and other terms that avoid specificity without forfeiting any clarity concerning what act he refers to. He says that he chooses not to have sex because he worries about having regrets and wants to make sure he does it with someone he likes.

Male #4, or "Marcus,"[19] is in a committed relationship, and most of his sex was had while in his three serious relationships. Most of his language is asymmetrical in the way Baker discusses: *fuck* is his preferred term in referring to the act, but when he speaks generally, his use seems to be gender-neutral. Men can fuck women, women can fuck men, and women can fuck and be fucked by women; his reference to the female "friend who fucked the girl, or got fucked by the girl" (lines 58–9)[20] shows his acknowledgement of the term's asymmetry, but it seems to be based on which party is the sexual aggressor rather than which is able to penetrate.

Male #5, or "Roy,"[21] has never been in a relationship and has had many partners. His answers usually deviate considerably from the questions asked, and he prefers speaking about specific people and situations to speaking about general feelings, opi-

---

17 We fucked a couple of times. It was just nice to hold someone. He wanted to make me feel good. He liked it rougher than I knew how to supply. I thought it was a game, trying to get him to fuck me, until I realized I was just playing with myself and he was game for anything. The fucking was just the beginning of his kindness. We remained friends for years until I moved and we lost touch.

18 Our friendship was a sad one: I think he wanted me to show him how to do sexual things, so he could have experience before he dated someone. Sad for him. Sadder for me, that I was that kind of resource, a go-to vagina.

19 He and I had sex hundreds of times.

20 That was me. I got fucked by the girl. I guess I was also the "friend" then, just that.

21 For the rest of college, rumor had it that I was the last girl he fucked. He called himself "bisexual" before he fucked me, and for not long after.

nons, or habits. He uses the terms *dick, cunt,* and *pussy.* He, too, more often uses *fuck* [22] than other terms for sex, and he does not use *hook up* except to refer to its use by others; the term has no place among his detailed and precise word choice. The term refers more to power and intent than to gender; when he speaks about his own desire or ability to fuck, he usually refers to sex with men.

Female #1, or "Misty," is in a committed relationship and recently ended another relationship, but she has also had a great deal of sex outside of relationships. She speaks very generally, tells no stories, mentions no specific acts or instances in which sex acts have happened, and generally avoids using language more specific than *hooking up* or *having sex.* Other language, such as "use what I've got" (line 172), "enjoy somebody else's company" (line 236), "behave like they're college students" (line 252), and "having a great time" (66) allow her to convey a sense of her open attitude without actually being open enough to use specific language and refer to example situations. Her lack of openness may be due to wariness associated with the bad reputation she speaks of.

Female #2, or "Danielle," has never had sex while in a relationship, and while she was quite sexually active at one time, she has not had sex recently. She enjoys telling stories, both hers and others', and many involve friends in relationships. She avoids using *fuck* or using slang terms for genitals; she says *slut* several times, but in a lighthearted way, referring to herself. [23]

Female #3, or "Val," [24] has had a few sex partners and has never been in a relationship, but she talks quite a bit about the *fuck buddies* she has had. When recounting her sexual encounters or talking about the practices of people she knows, she relies on the term *hook up* as a catch-all that can stand for most sex acts, useful when she wants to avoid being specific or is not privy to the information about other people that would allow her to be specific. She uses the word *slut* several times in explaining what she does not want people to say about her.

Female #4, or "Candice," is in a committed relationship and has had a few previous sex partners. She tells only one story, and it is about anal sex. Although she does

---

22 When we fucked, he went soft a couple minutes into it. He must have thought I would tell someone and then everyone would know, so, because offense is the best defense, he began tearing into me with incredible verbal cruelty within the hour.

23 *Slut* and *whore* are terms often applied to women who have sex with multiple partners. Cultural norms in today's American college communities dictate that young women should be closed-lipped, even ashamed, when divulging sexual histories if peers might label them "sluts."

24 We were best girlfriends. We were supposed to be closer than anyone. I've never had so much trouble understanding another person. I never saw what made her tick. I never even saw her shins.

not speak at length, she does not seem to be concealing anything or feeling shy—after all, she mentions a recent sexual encounter with her boyfriend in his office—but seems instead to be laid-back and without an interest in expressing strong opinions about sex.

Female #5, or "Alma,"[25] is in a new relationship. She has never had sex, but she is beginning to try new things with her boyfriend and expects to have sex with him soon. *Hooking up* and *doing things* are terms she uses to avoid being specific because she seems to feel uncomfortable about her lack of experience; however, the terms are not interchangeable, as the former is typically used when talking about casual encounters and does not apply to the sexual activity within her relationship. She mentions fellatio a few times, but otherwise remains vague when talking about sex acts. She has some experience with hooking up, and explains what she means by it; here, it seems to be used because it is part of her vocabulary rather than because she wants to conceal what she has done, but another factor may be the lack of terminology for the actions that have constituted "hooking up" in her experience. Her long wait to lose her virginity resulted from a long wait to meet and date a man she liked enough to have sex with; she has no problem with casual sex and expects to have it in the future, but did not want to lose her virginity during a casual encounter.

HOOKING UP

Every participant used the term *hook up*. All used the term at least once without prompting, except for Danielle, who used the term only once and in response to my question containing the term. Participants used the term in a general sense, as when Misty says, "You know who's hooking up with whom" (line 48), or in reference to specific incidents, as when Val says, "Me and him hooked up in the coatroom" (lines 270–1),[26] and occasionally to explain how their friends talk about sex, as when Jacob says, "But people'll be like, yeah, we—we hooked up or—or whatever" (lines 78–9).

"Or whatever" is an appropriate phrase to accompany *hook up* because of the imprecision of the term. Disagreement about what constitutes a hook-up can be seen in the definitions posted at UrbanDictionary.com. The definition most popular at the time of this writing specifies making out and having sex, but nothing else, as activities

---

25   Once I remembered who this girl was, I missed her terribly. She always seemed like a person who would continue to exist after college, which is probably why I never heard a word about her.

26   She talked about it a lot in the interview. I was a little jealous. I felt that I should've been the one to blow him, if I were the kind of girl who gave blow jobs, which I absolutely was not (I considered them degrading), because it sounded exciting.

that can be referred to using the term; the second most popular reads, "purposely am-
biguous, equivocal word to describe almost any sexual action. usually used to exagger-
ate or minimize what exactly happened. A hook-up can range from a make-out session
to full out sex."[27] Definition nine also acknowledges that hooking up "can range from
making out to sex and everything in-between."[28] Definition seventeen reads, "1. To get
one's dick wet. 2. Making out does not count."[29]

Interviewees, too, seemed to operate using differing definitions. Kyle seems to
separate hooking up from having sex when he says, "I've never hooked up, had sex, or
done anything to anyone when they were drunk" (lines 222–3),[30] and he aligns hooking up with kissing and designates both as acts less intimate than sex in saying, "Even
if it is just hooking up, just kissing or whatever, there is some sort of almost intimacy to
it" (lines 292–4). Theo uses *hook up* in line 12 to refer to a teammate having sex with
two girls, and Alma tells two stories at the beginning of the interview in which she
uses the term to refer to intercourse. Val uses the term in line 270 and then clarifies:
"Hooked up as in, we did a little oral action" (lines 275–6), and she later provides her
definition of the term:

> 373 hooking up? [yeah]
> 374 hooking up—
> 375 to me means—
> 376 anything fur—
> 377 I guess it includes—
> 378 making out.
> 379 hardcore making out—
> 380 um—
> 381 and further. after that.
> 382 oral. intercourse.
> 383 everything else—
> 384 um—it's a very loose term
> 385 that includes. a lotta things.

---

27 *UrbanDictionary.com*, s.v. "hook up," http://urbandictionary.com (accessed May 16, 2007).

28 Ibid.

29 Ibid; My best friend Stick was always talking about getting his dick wet, and I adopted this terminology, constantly talking about my need to get my dick wet. Sometimes I felt that if I actually did
have a dick, my life would be so much richer, because I would be sticking bitches all the time.

30 Before we fucked for the first time, we were at a party and I started to pour myself a drink. "If
you want to fuck tonight," he said, "you won't drink that." So I didn't.

Only one other interviewee, Alma, spoke of acts other than intercourse and kissing in providing her definition of the term:

173 I'll like randomly

174 like hook. up with guys?

175 but like not—

176 like I won't like.

177 do anything with their penis

178 unless like—

179 I'm more than just hooking.

180 like randomly hooking up with them

181 but like I'll just like make out

182 and boobs I.

183 don't matter to me

184 so like that kinda stuff <laughing>

No other participants attempted to list activities that constitute a hook-up. Both dictionary definitions quoted above refer to *hook up* as applying to a "range" of activities from making out to intercourse, and Val speaks of activities "further" beyond making out, such as oral sex and intercourse. Jacob labels "spooning" and "hardcore snuggling" as "precursors to sex" (lines 350–5),[31] suggesting a spectrum.

In the same way that *have sex* can be used with or without reference to another participant besides the subject, *hook up* can be used with or without an object. In this sense, the term has the grammatical symmetry Baker discusses—"Jane hooked up with Dick" is the same as "Dick hooked up with Jane." However, the term seems to also be symmetrical in the way that Moulton argues *have sex* is not: I find no evidence of a sense that hooking up is accomplished by an active party and a passive one. This is in part due to the term's ability to encompass a number of sexual acts without specifying one, and if the act is unclear, any actor or acted-upon party is even more difficult to determine. When Marcus says, "A friend of mine hooked up with a girl who is also a girl" (lines 9–11), he conceals or fails to mention what transpired during the encounter,

---

31 Anal sex does not fit into this spectrum, and seven interviewees (four male and three female) mentioned anal sex or anal stimulation as curious practices, or as practices thought to be curious by others. It is almost as though anal sex is thought to be something that happens among adults rather than college students.

and because even the act is unknown,[32] an assessment of symmetry can be based only on grammar and not content.

In some instances, *hook up* is surrounded by language that indicates the asymmetry of the action itself. The story Theo relates about a friend is an example:

> 12   he sorta hooked up with two girls
> 13   at the same time—and—
> 14   y'know he sorta finished with one girl—
> 15   but um—y'know by the time uh—
> 16   the sec- he got to the second girl.
> 17   she was really upset with him.

The man is the subject of the story, and he holds all the power in the situation: the two women function as stationary objects upon which he acts, as he finishes with one and gets to the other. The symmetry of the term used to set up the scenario becomes overpowered by the asymmetry of the behavior, or of the speaker's conception of the behavior.

Generally, interviewees' usage of *hook up* was limited. I hypothesized that participants would use the term to refer to sexual activity of which they did not know specific details, and I noted only one instance of this: Val spoke of "the girl he's hooking up with right now" (line 348), expressing knowledge of the general sexual situation without knowing what activities the sexual relationship consists of. As I expected, *hook up* was used to avoid revealing details, but only Val used it in this way:

> 270   um. me and him hooked up—
> 271   in the coatroom—
> 272   <laughing> of a party
> 273   um—
> 274   hooked up as in—
> 275   <laughs> we did a little oral action—

---

32   Both Marcus and Val attempted to slyly insert comments about an anonymous, dick-seeking, promiscuous, crazy, briefly-lesbian friend of theirs, seemingly thinking that rules of ethical conduct coinciding with the presence of a recording device would prevent the interviewee from acknowledging what had been said. Here's me acknowledging what he just said: this "friend of mine [who] hooked up with a girl who is also a girl" was me. My friend fed me Sparks and then ate me out against a bathroom door at a party, next to an overflowing toilet. Then she went downstairs and immediately told the lesbians what she'd done, wanting to be accepted as one of them.

Her halting delivery and nervous laughter,[33] the oblique language used even when she specifies the act, and the revision of the original statement indicate that she hesitated to disclose details but changed her mind. While the use of *hook up* is called for in a variety of situations, its appeal lies in its ability to preserve ambiguity, whether the motivation is maintenance of privacy, hesitance to speak of the unknown, or desire to speak generally about a variety of unspecified acts.[34]

HAVING SEX, MAKING OUT, FUCKING, AND MUNCHING PUSSY

The majority of the participants' references to sexual activity took the form of terms for intercourse; most popular were *have sex (with), sleep with, do (it) with/to,* and *fuck.* When referring to sexual acts other than intercourse, interviewees did not rely solely on *hook up* as a catch-all term: *do things,* and variations of that term, were popular when acts were not named. Often, using a particular term for an act (*blow,* for example) meant forfeiting not only ambiguity but also the sense of symmetry and equal agency afforded by the use of *hook up.* While most participants relied on the use of grammatically symmetrical terms, two preferred the decidedly asymmetrical *fuck.*

The most frequently used term for engaging in intercourse was, predictably, *have sex.* The term often appears without an object, referring instead to an action that could potentially be performed. Alma, for example, speaks of her roommates, two of whom "aren't having sex" (line 106).[35] The appearance of the term without an object can indicate symmetry in another sense, when the people having sex with each other are both the subject, as when Danielle says, "She and her boyfriend, like, had some crazy sex" (lines 43–4) and when Marcus says, "These two fat people I know had sex" (line

---

33 She aspired to be slutty like me. She wanted to have a number like mine, and then higher, much higher. She wanted to fuck everyone. She couldn't. She was afraid to be a girl. Never, ever wore skirts. How could anyone find the girl under all that cotton?

34 Grinding till he accidentally comes on my belly; making out in my bathroom after I puke up Vanilla Smirnoff; fingering on the couch in the afternoon; having to give head; sixty-nine in the master bedroom of the ski house; a foot rub?; friendly tonguing; a backrub that turns into some fucking; grinding in the radio station by the control board; again and again and again getting him (them) hard in my bed; never, ever holding hands.

35 At the time of this paper's writing, spring of senior year, I was not having sex. Nobody would have sex with me. Nobody would date me, either. I weighed between 115 and 120 pounds, either underweight or a couple of pounds away, with scrawny arms and sunken eyes and short-cropped hair. And I was batshit crazy. I would go to bars every night in nearly no clothes, hoping that someone would recognize my instability and decide to take advantage of me. One boy came home with me. He was sweet. I kissed him and then he went soft and went home. He didn't need to go. I didn't need to be fucked. I wanted to be kissed and held, and wanted my touched body to be rendered real, not the physical lie I suspected it to be, angles that could not exist, all padding curiously lacking.

21).[36] In both examples, both parties are actors. In other instances, there simply exists no evidence that either party is active and the other passive: Misty says, "Basically, like, I would have sex with people" (lines 130–1), Danielle speaks of "a friend who was having sex with her boyfriend in her car" (lines 116–7), and Candice mentions "having sex with, um, my boyfriend in his office" (lines 46–7). Switching the subject and object in each sentence does result in a difference in meaning, but this is not a result of imbalances in power; by default, the speaker (or the party with a relationship with the speaker) would be the sentence's subject and the other party would be the object. To switch those would be a deliberate and meaningful choice.

That such a transformation is possible is indicative of the ability of *have sex* to take on the role of an asymmetrical term. Two examples of this best exemplify speakers' ability to define an actor and an acted-upon and in doing so turn an expression of equal agency into one that applies to an imbalance in sexual power. Kyle states,

221 I've never hooked up had sex.
222 or done anything to anyone when they were drunk
223 or when I was drunk—

The placement of "had sex" alongside "done anything to," coupled with the phrases' context, defines an active party (the speaker) and a passive party. He speaks of personal responsibility here, and initially assigns the other party the passive role because of his or her impaired state, which creates an imbalance of power. Theo also places himself in the role of actor:

165 I mean. the last time I.
166 the last girl I didn't have sex with uh.
167 she was my girlfriend at
168 well not my girlfriend well—
169 she later became my girlfriend
170 she wasn't quite my girlfriend then but uh—
171 we y'know we didn't have sex because—
172 like. she's. she's v—
173 I knew she would regret it like.

---

36 Marcus always tried to be callous after our breakup. One day he rubbed my back, pressing hard into my bones, stripped of any fat, and said, "Your back used to be perfect." He was one of the kindest men I had ever known and he had to cover that up with ten layers of vitriol, like peach slices wrapped in tinfoil.

174 she definitely tried to get me to have sex with her

175 and I knew that like later she would

176 she'd regret it—

177 so I just. didn't let it happen—

Most striking here is his assessment of their roles when he says, "She definitely tried to get me to have sex with her" (line 174). The woman is subject to his decisions and sexual power, but he chooses to refrain from activity. Without the ability to act, the woman can only attempt to instigate. None of the interviewees spoke of themselves in a passive role; no statements such as "He had sex with me" appeared.[37]

The asymmetry possible in the use of *have sex* is more nuanced than that of *fuck*, which Moulton argues is inherently asymmetrical.[38] The interviewees' usage was often consistent with this idea; there seemed to exist a general awareness of the term's asymmetry, but it was not tied to the ability of the man to penetrate the woman, only of one party to act as sexual aggressor. Jacob is aware that "beefy men" speak of sex in a "crude" way, as in, "fuck bitches, y'know, come on this, come on that" (lines 161–6).[39] Marcus uses *fuck* with the frequency that most other participants use *have sex*,[40] but he is aware of its inherent asymmetry, evident in his reference to "the [female] friend who fucked the girl—or got fucked by the girl" (lines 57–9); since the notion of the fucker and the fucked here has nothing to do with a penis and vagina, he considers instead the aggression or instigation of one party.

---

37 The boy who raped me had sex with me: that was my whole problem. That was my obsession. None of this insanity would have happened if I'd stayed a virgin just a little longer, met Marcus a little sooner, been less fucked from the outset of my sexual history.

38 At the beginning of the semester during which I wrote this paper, I saw my rapist again. I'd been thinking about him all the time. I was sure that I would never see him again because in my head he was so monstrous that he was barely real. Then I saw him sitting on McKeldin Mall on a nice day. I'd only seen him once since I cut off contact—he had held the door for me as I entered Susquehanna Hall, and I didn't acknowledge him—but I tracked him via Facebook to make sure I knew what he was up to. Then he was real. I'm sure he was looking right at me. I texted and called Val in distress. She told me to stop bothering her with my drama. Stick came over, and I never said what was wrong, and had never told him about the rape, but of course he knew. I feel like we didn't leave my couch for days.

39 My rapist was not a beefy man. He was exactly one inch shorter than me, of average build with a beer belly, not muscular. But he did fuck this bitch. He came on this belly, came in this mouth, came in this cunt.

40 Marcus was used to saying *fuck* around me; after all, he and I had practically been married for a year and had fucked hundreds of times. I think we'd both say it was as symmetrical as vaginally dry, Astroglide-aided, rape trauma-hindered missionary sex can be. How could we ever fuck like normal people? We began dating about a month after I was raped. The rapist and I were still "dating" at the time. Marcus gently suggested, later, that I had been raped. I said he was wrong. He wanted me to stop being sad. He and I did love each other very much, symmetrically.

Other acts, some of which constitute hooking up and some that do not, were named during the interviews. Naturally, specificity is sometimes required by the topic, such as Val's statement that "giving head after college is weird" (lines 483–4).[41] Jacob brings up "the shocker," defined as "two in the pink, one in the stink" (lines 16 and 23), and remarks that it is an inappropriate act to perform with a person one is "just randomly like hooking up with sexually" (lines 33–4). Roy speaks at length about a sexual encounter between his acquaintance and a man she met at a bar:

83   he like ate her out
84   on her fridge <Elissa laughs>
85   like she has this like
86   outdoor freezer thing
87   and she got on top of it
88   and took her jeans off
89   and then he was like
90   lickin' her pussy and then
91   she started like—
92   um. y'know
93   laughing too hard
94   so then they went inside they—
95   and she still made out
96   she she. he went
97   cunt to mouth but. <laughs>
98   yeah. he was he was eatin'—
99   munchin' away and
100 then like she tells me all about
101 how he munched away again.

Although this encounter seems to meet the criteria of a hook-up, it is difficult to determine so because he does not use the term. However, the passage is noteworthy when considered alongside Murnen's argument that men use more aggressive and degrading language when referring to sex and women's genitals. Roy's use of *cunt* here can certainly be thought of as use of degrading language, and this language and its connotations relating to the woman's power would be absent if the story were colapsed

---

41 Giving head in a coatroom after college would be weird. So many of the escapades described in these interviews would be weird if done after college, I realize now. But giving head now, after getting some practice, is less weird than before.

and encapsulated by *hook up*. Accompanying the detail lost when the phrase appears is a reduction of the sense of a skewed sexual power dynamic.[42]

CONCLUSION

The rise in popularity of the term *hook up* and its entry into the lexicon of the typical University of Maryland undergraduate student have shaped it into a highly nuanced term that may appear to be all-purpose in reference to casual sexual encounters, but its usage sometimes conceals information, sometimes stands in place of unknown or unspecified information, and sometimes stands in for a term the speaker does not feel comfortable using.[43] The asymmetry of *fuck*, *have sex*, and similar terms Baker and Moulton described in the 1970s remains today,[44] and *hook up* fits into the models they present. However, women's increased sexual autonomy[45] has allowed them to fit into the role of sexual aggressor, and therefore allowed them to fuck, lessening the applicability of arguments about usage based in roles linked to cultural conceptions of anatomy. In an environment in which casual oral sex performed in a bathroom or on an outdoor freezer is acceptable, if not commonplace, attitudes about sexual roles have unsurprisingly shifted to allow Jane to fuck Dick just as Dick can fuck Jane.[46]

---

42 It's hard to say what I was trying to argue here. Really, I think I just wanted to wedge in the story about Jillian getting eaten out on a fridge.

43 Whereas some of us are so damaged that we say, *I fucked*, we say, *look at the channels I've carved into my insides over time*, we say, *this is exactly what I did, in and out, I turn my insides outward to you, I'll show you a level of bedroom insanity you've never imagined, and I dare you to talk shit, because when you do, you will help me to spread my reputation far and wide, and soon the whole world will know that I am no ingénue: I'm so thoroughly fucked raw and hardened over that no one will ever penetrate me again.*

44 Thus, I would never say "Elissa did it to Damian," although I would tell myself too many times during long nights, examining my emotional fracture lines, "Damian did it to Elissa." Again, Damian bangs Elissa, Elissa does not bang Damian; Damian humps Elissa, Elissa does not hump Damian. Damian comes in Elissa's mouth and after she meets him, for a year, Elissa can barely even come when she's alone, in the dark, with a pillow over her head. Would it be outside the scope of this conversation to ask whether Damian rapes Elissa? Or is that what this discourse analysis was about all along?

45 She can do what she wants, fuck who she wants. She can wash her lithium down with vodka and soda water, wear nearly nothing against the DC winter, take on a fuck buddy, show him tricks he'll know she's learned somewhere and performed on someone, reach under the bed for her stash of condoms and lube without having to look, insist she feels nothing. She can be as free as she wanted to be as a teenager reading *Cosmo*, planning for future satisfaction of her voracious sexual appetite. She can fuck everything that walks. It'll be great.

46 And before that stung, smarting girl knows it, the manic pain will seem outdated, and the need for liberation will disappear, because she'll be all grown up.

A Cascade Autobiography

PART 10

I felt compelled to make up for my diluted blood because some concentrated proof had to exist to make me Indian. In the absence of blood quantum, culture, and tradition, I called upon my book smarts. I studied legislation and Supreme Court cases and read about Indians with guns taking over buildings back when my dad had long hair and drove a VW Bug. Even though I never needed it, I carried my tribal card in my wallet. Once I moved to Seattle, I began to feel that I could leave it at home with my unstamped passport. At the University alone, there were hundreds of other Native people who I might meet at any time—intentionally, if I wanted to—so I ceased to feel as I did during so many DC area conversations, like an artifact whose authenticity is being evaluated for inclusion in a museum.

During my second year of grad school, I attended a Native graduate research symposium at my University and felt comfortable, because none of us, even the white-looking ones, were pretending. I had achieved a new kind of belonging: a comfort with a split ethnic identity. Once I moved to Seattle and people stopped questioning, I realized that, sure, I am Native, but I am also very, very white.

Dear Diary, Part 2

9/18/07, 8:41 a.m.

I'm all moved into my apartment in Seattle. I have been for a couple weeks. My parents and I drove across the country. Now I'm all alone and the akathisia is so intense. I can't read, or do anything really. I miss my parents so much. I feel like they took half my organs with them when they drove back East.

It's another hour till the mall opens and I can spend my pain away. Things have not been good. I've gotten into this horrible routine: wake up, maybe go to gym, eat, watch pirated *Law & Order* DVDs, drive somewhere to buy things, come home and feel rotten, eat, spend the evening talking on the phone and going online and moping before going to bed around nine. I check the mail many times during the day. Even after I have already picked it up.

Tonight I should probably go to the Melvins show downtown but I think I am too depressed to do that or anything else.

Last night the phone kept ringing and it was this telemarketing thing. It was torture. It's hard enough to get to sleep these days, with my guts in a snake.

I can't wait till things start happening next week. Grad school starting and my student insurance starting, so I can go see the new psychiatrist about all these feelings.

9/23/07, 1:30 a.m.

I'm starting to figure out why I'm supposed to love Seattle. And remember why I am supposed to love everything.

9/24/07, 1:29 p.m.

My new psychiatrist is way different from my old one. She got my life history and treatment history, decided Dr. R. messed up my meds. She scolded me for taking both Klonopin and Ativan and said to throw away the Ativan. Yeah, right. She's starting me on Seroquel. Now I can't have any more Ativan and I'm upset about it because I need it.

10/10/07, 6:44 p.m.

I feel like my head got some ventilation. The Seroquel is working out. We put me on a very low dose of Lexapro (antidepressant I used to be on) too, and now all of a sudden I can read, I can sleep, think, and my psychic pain doesn't feel like a marinade anymore. They say you're supposed to go back to your "old self." I thought that was cheesy. Sure it is. But it's true. No clouds on my brain, no blankets, wet towels—Seroquel is like shearing sheep. Pulling off the strangeness. I read back and think of all the thoughts, the extra thoughts that used to be in my head that I needed to get out. All the thoughts are gone. Bipolar disorder is hyperactivity. Dear God, please, please don't let it come back.

10/30/07, 9:06 a.m.

So last night Callie and I were on our way back here after going to the bar, when Stacey called to tell me our friend Henry killed himself. My response was to just get angry and start ranting about how it was my fault. Callie and I got back here and sat around and ripped up this coaster that a guy had written his phone number on. There are still little mounds of pieces on the floor.

Henry called me a bunch of times over the past month. Things were going really badly. Once he called me while I was at a party and then called back while I was at a bar. He told me he was about to kill himself and that I should not settle for guys who treat me like shit. I let him go because I knew he wasn't going to do anything.

The last time I talked to him was on Saturday. He said his gf was pissed at him because some girl told him she loves him. He sounded okay, though, so I let him go when my cousin called to say she was ready to pick me up.

Killing yourself is a lot of work. It's less work when you have a bottle of Klonopin and a bottle of gin. But I didn't think he was going to do anything.

When things were good, we used to talk about fragrances. He got me a little vial of Dior Homme when I couldn't stop talking about it.

He told me on the phone that he always had a crush on me. I didn't know what to do with that.

He was on medication and it never helped. It scares me—Dr. C. says we're at the end of the road, drug-wise. Just a couple weeks ago I was so fucking low I didn't know what to do with myself. Then up again. Lately there are ups, real ones, not manic ones, real spots of sky.

11/19/07, 12:18 p.m.

Usually I only post when I'm super depressed, but lately life has been pretty good, and I'm going to list all the ways how.

1. I just got a TV. This is the first TV I've had that never belonged to anybody else. I do not have cable. But I have a TV. And a DVD player. And Netflix.

2. My drugs seem to be working.

3. I'm not romantically interested in anyone right now. Well, I sort of have a crush, but I'm not planning to act on it, so it's just pleasant right now.

4. My nonfiction is really starting to shape up. Coming to this MFA program was a good idea.

5. I finished all my work for Amazon, and my next paycheck from them will probably be bigger than a whole summer's worth of paychecks from the desk.

The bad things:

1. I think stress is weakening my immune system and also giving me acne.

2. I'm gaining weight because I'm always fucking eating.

More good:

1. For the first time in fucking forever, the bad things are just not that bad at all.

12/8/07, 8:56 p.m.

I was just standing on the balcony, and I realized, I am really glad I'm here.

This quarter has been really rough. New place and all. And I complain about school a lot. And everything else.

But next quarter, I'm going to make it better. Being well is knowing that I have the ability to make it better.

1/14/08, 9:10 a.m.

One day I woke up and my brain was rotting. It was like when you're eating bread and halfway through you notice it's full of blue-green mold. One day I woke up and had been bipolar my whole life. I could tell everyone *I told you so* or *If we had done it differently*, but now I know I wouldn't have. I wouldn't choose sanity if I could. Sanity is smug. Insanity is vulnerable and self-aware.

That's easy to say now. My head is more like a hotel than a padded cell. A cabin in the woods.

Can't believe how much weight I've gained. It started with these $1 frozen meals, all carby and shit, then progressed to Indian food. Can't believe I don't care. I guess that's the trade-off—got my sanity back, plus 30 pounds. I look in the mirror and I think I recognize myself. Did I always look like this? I will think on it. More later.

A Cascade Autobiography

PART 11

At the Native research symposium I attended in grad school, I was fatiguing of heavy talk about colonization, subjugation, the white man, our people (as though we're all one people), the Creator, power structures and dominance, when a presenter brought me out of my free-sandwich-induced stupor by telling us that rape and genocide are intertwined. Sexual violence is a form of control and oppression, of course. Sexual violence is not only an attack on bodies, but on identity, humanity, and larger cultural groups of women. I started thinking about myself not only as a part of a Native community, but a different tribe, one of young women sucking on silence, biting down hard on their tongues, because putting out is normal, and no matter how much it hurts to be quiet, it hurts more to say something.

Having been raped as a virgin used to seem to have a lot in common with being Indian. People were skeptical and I didn't have enough proof. Both had to do with being fucked over. But Indianness is cool now, evidenced by the dreamcatchers spangling every rack at Urban Outfitters. Being a rape victim just sucked, for a while. Sometimes, though, without meaning to be, I was proud: I have suffered, and that entitled me to something, but I didn't know what. Everyone seems to be reaching deep into the crevices of their souls to find oozing gobs of pain, and if that pain was parented by some distant generation that spent brutal winters chasing diminishing herds after its own numbers had dwindled from the settler's diseases and brute force, it seems even more potent, wrapped around our DNA double-helixes. A pain so old begins to feel like predestination, locking every generation into more, whether that's the truth or something

93

I tell myself because I like the pain. Even more, I savor the twisted prestige of inheriting old hurts most people only read about in history books.

Sexually Based Offenses

The *Law & Order* franchise has permeated American culture so thoroughly that both times I was called in for jury duty, the judges' spiels to the potential jurors included the warning that we must not make the mistake of thinking the courtroom proceedings would be anything like *Law & Order.* Separating the King County Superior Court from the mahogany halls of the television crime drama was impossible for me, because I knew nothing else: I was close to turning six when the first episode premiered September 13, 1990, but I always skipped over the show while channel surfing until *Law & Order: Special Victims Unit* hit the airwaves when I was fourteen.

I have watched every episode of *Special Victims Unit,* most of them more than once, some many more times. I never cared for the original—vanilla, it's often called—and I felt that *Criminal Intent* went downhill long before it moved from NBC to USA. But *SVU* gets better with age. Every new rape is more gruesome and heart-wrenching than the last. Vanilla was canceled at the end of its twentieth season, while *SVU*'s ratings were still strong.

An episode goes like this: First, as the words *Law & Order* appear on the screen, a phantom guy's voice says, "In the criminal justice system, sexually based offenses are considered especially heinous. In New York City, the dedicated detectives who investigate these vicious criminals are members of an elite squad known as the *Special Victims Unit.* These are their stories." Then the *Law & Order* sound: *bomm bomm.*

Then the teaser, in which we meet the victim and crime scene—and the cops, of course. They say something kind of memorable to punctuate the scene, then there's the opening credits. Then the detectives at work. You think you know what's up, and then there's a twist, and the original perp is not the perp anymore. Then more solid detective work, new perp, then some legal stuff, which usually gets complicated, and usually a verdict, good or bad, and always, without fail, an ending that really makes you think.

SVU has even made its way into my dreams. No surprise, after thousands of minutes of rape, murder, justice, and the frustrating lack of it. I have re-watched many episodes, learning my lines. The crimes against me, the real-life ones, are without documentation. I didn't go to the cops. I forgot so much, but in the years following, I began to remember, always during waking hours, watering my cacti or stretching my leg across my bike frame. A sleuth for forgotten details, I watched for plot points that would remind me of me so I could tell myself I was a victim: that is how I worked to solve my own case.

I've dreamed of vics and perps, interrogation, making complaints that someone raped me or dismembered me or turned me into a zombie.

Each episode is a closed narrative: it begins, it ends. Case solved or not, the episode closes. Within each episode, we see the quest, the conflict, and the resolution. Within forty-two minutes, it's all cleaned up and DICK WOLF comes up on the screen to let you know that it's time to move along.

I've seen most of the episodes on TV, but after I got Netflix in grad school, I started watching them one after another, for hours, for days. After class, I'd come home, change into my New Jersey hoodie and flannel pants, and slouch down into my three-dollar desk chair, getting comfortable enough to stare at the laptop screen for hours. In my pink leather notebook, I scribbled lines from the show that reminded me of myself, as though I was a sleuth, solving my own case. At the end of every forty-two minute block, a problem was solved. Sometimes, the problem wasn't actually solved, but at least everyone knew there was a problem, and Detective Olivia Benson got that look on her face like she felt the rape to her core and would undo it if she could. I watched until I couldn't take it anymore, and then I went to bed and dreamed about it.

Once in a while, while watching, I'd pause the show to send my younger brother, Nate, instant messages. I let him know when Detective Elliot Stabler roughs up a suspect, or Detective John Munch makes a witty remark, or Ice-T shows his street cred. Nate, four years my junior, knows what happened to me: a year after the rape, I called my parents to tell them about what happened, and when Nate asked why they were upset, my dad shuffled the receiver to the side and said, "Elissa was raped." It seemed that he was trying to avoid secrecy and shame by keeping the thing out in the open, a gesture I appreciated. That conversation was the last we had about the issue. During my visits home, we would still watch the episodes together, taking in the brutality. They watched me watch: watched me get mad. Still, we didn't talk about it. Television being entertainment, we dutifully cheered for Stabler when he'd catch a perp, slam him against the wall and recite him the rights he didn't deserve. Before I was raped, none of this meant anything to us. Episode after episode, brutal rape after bloody murder, we were all enjoying ourselves.

I sought to watch until everything in my head, every doubt, every piece of fuzz obscuring some memory, would be replaced by Olivia's voice telling me that I was so, so strong. But I didn't feel strong, didn't feel that I had ever been, and those lines running through my head were water against my oily memory. But then they clotted, and I thought about how it might have been if I'd talked, or how my story could be portrayed in episode form, neat, sectioned, with closure. Three years after the rape, I took all those scratches from my pink notebook, typed them into neat lines, and plugged them into a grid that made sense to me, with lines from the show on one side, pinned up against my true story on the other:

SVU	ELISSA
BAD COP: Why didn't you report him?	
	For a while I didn't know whether I had been raped. I never asked for anyone's opinion. I didn't call the cops. Sometimes I wish I had. I think all the time about what I should've said. If I had called the cops, none of this not-believing-me bullshit would go on like it does.
BAD COP: Tell me what happened. From the beginning. Don't leave *anything* out.	
	So I met him online. I was in the middle of a breakup with my high school boyfriend and this guy and I hit it off okay. After all this time, I can remember his weird smile. It seemed cute then. Now it's just gross.
BAD COP: An intact hymen. The vic is a virgin.	

I told him we had to take it slow. I wasn't ready for sex. Maybe eventually, but not now. He had a temper. He made me do things. Like he'd jack off onto my belly and throw me a towel. Make me suck his dick and then brush my teeth. I remember being scared of him the night he punched the wall.

BAD COP:

Look, rape is a serious charge. Do you understand what rape is? Did you tell him to stop? I got *real* victims to hand-hold and walk through the system.

It was 3 a.m. on my mother's birthday, 2005. This was in Maryland. I was twenty.

BAD COP:

You are responsible too. You chose to sleep with him. You chose to have sex without a condom. You chose a risk the same way you could've chosen to say no.

I don't know why we were sleeping in the same bed, naked. I guess he wanted to. I woke up with his weight on me. He was kind of small but still heavy like a bag of bricks. Of course I said no. People ask about that, as if I didn't say no. I definitely said no.

GOOD COP:

We all do what we have to. You have *nothing* to be ashamed of. Nobody

has the right to touch you. You did
very well. You did, you survived.

It felt like there were spikes in there.

BAD COP:

Why not just fight back? Predictions
of violence are notoriously unreli-
able. Nobody can say what he might
have done. Did you ever say no?

*I remember thinking, okay, I could
shove him off me. But he throws things,
punches things sometimes, and now he's
got me pinned.*

VILLAIN:

The expression on a girl's face her
first time is... incomparable. A girl's
virginity would be the ultimate col-
lectible, wouldn't it?

*I guess I was also thinking, let's get this
over with. Go ahead, break me in. I was
so tight and my muscles worked against
him. It took him a while to get all the
way in. I went ahead and let him do it
because I was thinking, next time will
be easier.*

VILLAIN:

She said no, but she just lay there. I
plucked her. She went limp. Like she
wanted to be punished. Then I took
her. I think she liked it. What do
you think?

*He fell asleep and I didn't. I was bleed-
ing. I threw him out in the morning. He
was so angry that he didn't say a single
word. I went to the university health*

center for the morning-after pill. The nurse practitioner thought this boy may have taken advantage of me.

GOOD COP:

We know the moment victims talk about what happened is the moment they start to heal. Maybe one day you can forgive yourself when you realize it wasn't your fault.

She was so nice to me, but I hated her guts, and I grabbed a handful of free condoms from the basket on her desk just to show her.

GOOD COP:

Date rape is a problem on every campus.

I never thought about calling the cops. I mean, not until it was way too late. What I knew about rape came from SVU: man is bad, woman says no, man fucks her anyway. What kind of episode would "No—well, okay, maybe, since you're in there anyway" make? So I decided to forget whatever violation I thought went down and make a relationship out of it.

BAD COP:

Making an accusation of rape is pretty drastic, don't you think? Women who have sex and later regret it are not entitled to call their partners rapists.

I thought I could make myself fall in love with him and that would fix it. I know, it's fucked up, it's stupid. But fuck you if you think it means I wanted it.

BAD COP:

It seems like everyone's a victim of something these days. She probably watched too many "women in jeopardy" movies. I'm not saying there aren't terrified women in need of protection. But there are a lot of vindictive ones who abuse the system. I think your alleged victim is one of them.

I know how it would've been if I'd gone to the police with this. I bled in the bathroom with my back against the door because there was no lock on it. I told myself I'd become a woman by fire.

BAD COP:

Nobody is blaming her, but we all know how hard it is to get an indictment on a he-said-she-said even without the ambiguities. An innocent victim? Very rare.

VILLAIN:

She does whatever I tell her to do. Whatever I say, whatever I want. And in the end, two little words will set me free: reasonable doubt.

Bad guys do what good guys dream.

I had sex with him four more times. It made me feel like a grown-up. It was also hard to turn him down. One night, I told him over the phone that I wasn't going to see him anymore but he said he was outside my building. Another night, my roommate let him in.

Those other times, I screamed, pretended I liked it. I wanted him to come so I wouldn't have to finish him off with my mouth. I guess I was just trying to convince myself I was into it.

GOOD COP:

Over half a million women are raped in this country every year. And only a fraction of them report it. Because they're too ashamed. It's a really screwed up world. But it's not your fault. And what happened to you? Doesn't make you the monster.

Even though he sucked, even though he's the scum of the earth, back then I would've rather let him ruin my life then put something into motion that would ruin his, too. He was my only friend.

ASSISTANT DISTRICT ATTORNEY:

Do you know how the law defines rape in the first degree? Sexual intercourse through forcible compulsion.

I felt like he forced me. What counts as force? Should he have punched me in the face? Held a knife against my throat?

GOOD COP:

I have never known a single victim who regretted testifying against a rapist, no matter how hard it was, but I have known plenty that wish that they had. And by then it was too late.

How could I have gone to the police? I said no and then yes. Nothing else matters. No and yes are the most important words in the world.

GOOD COP:

You expect her to come forward when most women won't.

I met a new guy and fell in love with him. I told the rapist we were through and he sent me a bunch of nasty text messages, all of them calling me a slut. I went on to fuck a bunch of other men. I didn't really like most of them but it was nothing personal.

GOOD COP:

By acknowledging that it affects you: that's the way you handle something traumatic.

I called the university help line and the man said I wasn't raped, that women who are raped are beaten up, sometimes they die.

GOOD COP:

Going through a rape kit, testimony, cross examination can be hard. Some women just wanna move on.

I went to a counselor and she said I did what I had to do to save myself but I knew that wasn't true.

GOOD COP:

I think you need to remember what kind of woman you are. And *get pissed off.* Or you're gonna be a victim for the rest of your life.

It took me a year to use the word "force." Another couple months to use "rape." Using these words has become privileged. Fuck everyone who made it so, fuck the idea of crying wolf, and fuck the day I was born tight, pretty, and eager to please.

VILLAIN:

Rape's the worst crime there is. Do you know why?

COP:

Tell me.

VILLAIN:

Let's look at twin sisters. Both beautiful, both smart, and a man is going to ask one out on a date. The only difference is, one of them was raped. So, who's the man going to ask out?

COP:

I don't think it matters.

VILLAIN:

Oh, but it does. Once you know, you know.

COP:

Doesn't matter if you care.

VILLAIN:

Really.

VILLAIN:	
I'm fixed on you, and until I'm dead, I'll always be in your head. We're joined at the hip now. Aren't we?	*He told me I was going to remember him forever because he was my first. See how right he was?*

- -

Scene. But we're not even close to the episode's end. There has to be a twist. When Vanilla premiered in 1990, its episodes were customarily separated, to some degree, into ORDER (the first half), meaning cops, and LAW (the second half), meaning lawyers. *SVU* doesn't really function this way—it's a mess of vics and perps and lawyers and cops the whole way through. Generally speaking, the lawyers do mostly inhabit the latter part of the episode. I know all their legalese. It convinced me that there never would've been any point in me going to the cops.

In my case, the twist came in the form of another man shrouded in dark shadow in the night, trailing behind him every *Law & Order* line I'd recorded in my notebook and leaving me unsure whether I had turned the show into reality or myself into fiction.

- -

BAD COP:

Tell us about Friday night.

Six weeks ago, just short of three years after the rape, my dad's birthday this time, something else happened. I live in Seattle now. My friend thought I would hit it off with her boyfriend's buddy. We met up with him at a bar.

He was older than me and he had a kid but I tried to keep an open mind. I'm not exactly an awesome judge of character, but it still wasn't that hard to see he was creepy.

BAD COP:

She's drinking apple martinis to try to lose control and he's drinking Amstel Lights to try to keep it. You gonna tell me she's not flirting with him?

GOOD COP:

Doesn't mean she asked to be raped.

BAD COP:

Not exactly the poor, fragile victim we thought she was.

GOOD COP:

'Cause she's not wearing panties, you mean?

I have this policy: no drunk sex, ever. Another policy: no visible panty lines.

VILLAIN:

She was a slut, that one, a real little whore. Hey, she gets around, what else am I supposed to call her? Plus, she wasn't exactly dressed in her refusal outfit. I saw the opportunity, and I took it.

We went to my friend's boyfriend's place so the creep could sober up on the couch till he was ready to give me a ride

BOOKSTORE

him to do me. I re-
me.

Thank you fo
Midtown Sc

h and he put his
nd then half his
be was looking for
e box. He took out
and wrapped my
my hand didn't
y body over, came
d against me.

twist, and pull
in middle school,
or some reason I
ive, so I shut up.
For a little while, I was in his possession.

VILLAIN:

The thing was exquisite. It's like
putting an animal down. You have
to disassociate. She was beside herself. She yelped like a whipped dog.

There's beauty in everyone. Sometimes you have to dig deep to find it.

But then I snapped out of it and said, no, not without a condom. So he was like, I assure you, I've had a vasectomy and I'm clean. I was like, Fine but I don't believe you. He asked why not, I said I don't trust men. Wanted to know when he had the vasectomy, he said age twenty-two. Why'd they let you get it so young? I asked. Personal problem, he told me. Sorry, I said, but I won't have sex without a condom. Why don't you trust men? he wanted to know. I told him I was raped. He asked, The kind where you said no or the kind where you regretted it?

PSYCHIATRIST:

Likes the sound of his own voice. He can do no wrong, nothing is his fault. No empathy, no conscience, no thought for the possible consequences of his actions. It's not about intimacy, it's about displaced rage. He hates women. But he likes humiliation and control. It's not about attraction, or power, or dominance, it's about annihilation.

So, in the end, he didn't penetrate me. I'm supposed to be happy about that, like what I got was nothing. Look how happy I am.

VILLAIN:

What's the difference between a slut and a bitch? A slut will screw anything, and a bitch will screw anything but you.

It's like a game. Will she, won't she. And if she says no? Plenty of fish in the sea.

I went upstairs to puke at some point. He ate me out at some point. Let's try this, I think he said. I don't know what happened after I passed out. Probably nothing, I hope.

DEFENSE ATTORNEY:

Please. There was never penetration.

I remember thinking during the thing that he had a voice like a serial killer from Special Victims Unit. *Low, scary. Even. Calm, I guess. I was thinking, if this were TV, would his character kill my character right now? The camera would have been behind the couch, I thought, pointed past our heads into the darkness, catching the curl of his lip, the terrified parting of mine, and the light from the street illuminating our polarized expressions.*

I woke up around six. I was alone but I was scared he was still around. I put on my boots and my coat and ran out of the apartment, ran a couple blocks, called a cab. I cried in the cab, called my friend from across the continent, and asked him how the hell this happened to me again, like some god-damn lightning striking twice.

BAD COP:

Rape is a violation of body and mind. A violation that comes through penetration. If you weren't raped and there's no evidence of assault, then there's not a lot we can do.

There was probably no evidence. Maybe if I had been raped again I would've called the cops, but I wasn't, so I didn't, I just went home and locked myself in my apartment for three days, thinking, fuck rapists, fuck that creep, fuck police who can't do anything without fluid evidence, and fuck Elissa Washuta's existence.

DEFENSE ATTORNEY:

Our complaining witness appears to have a history of emotional problems. Could a manic episode lead her to act out sexually? You put her on the stand, I'll be forced to bring up her promiscuity. It's her word against his.

I've done things with my body, consensually, that I am ashamed to admit. I don't think I'm allowed to complain about being touched, not anymore. I guess I went out looking to get fucked. That's what I always did. So I deserved everything I got. And anyway, wasn't this inevitable? Hadn't I always known that the first time unbound me, opened me up for more? I had been waiting for my next pillaging. It was only a matter of time.

GOOD COP:

That sounds like a terrible ordeal.

BAD COP:

What do you want, a medal?

My friend who introduced us said she was sorry about what happened to me, but I don't think she knew how bad I felt. I didn't give her the details.

DEFENSE ATTORNEY:

No judge would ever let this go before a jury. There is no case here. Why are we even debating this? My client has done nothing illegal, so good luck getting an indictment. There were no signs of a struggle in that room. Where's the crime? What you know about the law could fit in the palm of my hand. Forget him, girl, he'll bury you.

Plus I guess I knew I wouldn't have a case. And I can't handle it when someone questions me. I can scream "fuck you" a million times to my pillow, but could never say it to the face of a doubter. It's not really worth it to pursue this in court. I don't think I'd feel any better if he got punished.

I keep thinking, if it were anyone but me, someone who guarded her box, didn't spread her legs for men whose

faces she can't remember now, it would
be different.

VILLAIN:

Hey, tiger: let's do this again some-

time.

You want drama? Want a story? Here's the story RAINN (Rape, Abuse & Incest National Network) tells: in this country, only 40% of rapes are reported and 6% of rapists do time; two-thirds of rapes are committed by someone the victim knows; one in six of our women has been the victim of rape or attempted rape, making that seventeen million of us. In the "The More You Know" NBC public service announcement done by Mariska Hargitay (who plays Benson on *SVU*), she says, "If you've ever been a victim of rape, don't remain silent. It's never too late to get help."

As if it weren't painful enough to lay on a couch with the spins, not sure whether the vomit that threatens to come up is from the booze or the repulsion, hating myself for putting myself back in this situation (because girls are always taught that we're responsible for the situations we end up in), hurting from the vaginal canal out, I was tortured by the special pain of wondering whether the immediate experience of Brian's grimy, smoke-stained hand inside of me was less real than the plot points I had jotted down during my *SVU* marathon-watching sessions. But at least I could close my eyes and see familiar characters' faces instead of memorizing the movements of his hands spreading my thighs. I retain few mental images of that night, and for that, you'd think I'd feel fortunate, but really, I spent years vexed by the notion that if I can't see it in my head the way I can see *SVU* in my head, it never really happened.

It's a good thing that growing up means growing out of your old self, old body. Like a cicada's brittle brown shell. When you molt, there's green underneath, iridescent, so brilliant it's like you'll never turn hard and dark again.

VILLAIN:

The women victims, for the most

part, were asking for it. They take

our manhood, they suck us dry,

they mess with our heads—and
then they're surprised when we
fight back. People think sex offend-
ers are different. We're like aliens.
Drooling fiends lurking in the bush-
es. We're just like everybody else.

*I'm not afraid to walk alone at night.
I'm not afraid of being assaulted again.
I tell myself, next time, I'm calling the
cops for damn sure. But I've been telling myself that for five years.*

ASSISTANT DISTRICT ATTORNEY:

She ran to a different city, she ran
from man to man trying to find
comfort. And finally, she sat here
and relived every sordid, painful
detail. Her sex life dissected. Her
psychological traumas exposed.
Her entire motivation called into
question. So ask yourselves this:
Why would she put herself through
such hell if she wasn't telling the
truth?

COP:

It will kill you. Every horror, every
torment afflicts your body like a
cancer. It's devouring you and you
can't see it. Open your eyes.

*I have a nice life. I take five pills a day
to keep my moods straight. I don't think
about jumping in front of a train anymore. Maybe I should have done things
differently, but, you know, I'm fine. I
don't need to see a therapist, call a help
line, because I've got it together. My life
is the best it ever was.*

And then black, and then credits, and then the other side stretches out long and dark across the continent, enveloping Maryland and New Jersey and Seattle, coursing through every meeting with the boys who say "Suck it" when I don't and "Shut up, bitch" when I won't, the boy who doesn't think I deserve the waste of a condom and leaves me looking and feeling like I've been rubbed in gravel, the one who fucks me and steals my credit card, the one who pulls a knife and hides a gun, the dear friend who touches me even when I beg him not to and who cries later when he tries to understand what he's done—these boys exist in that black-screen space. They are the aftermath that television suggests and real life provides. But alongside these psychic stab wounds, I've got what television can barely suggest: the self-repair that my brain performs in the years after the detectives would have moved on.

After so much denial and anger, those first two haunts of the grieving heart, I found that it was time to progress. Being intact again, that alluring prize at the end of recovery, presents the scariest reality of all, the one that makes me wish I was hurting again: if this source of my pain is gone, but I still double over, what the hell is wrong with me? When it stops coming from the lingering wounds left by someone else's brute force, my own mental violence is all that's left to blame.

Bomm bomm. And then the next stage of grief came, and I bargained with every devil, asking to forget again. I watched until there was some hope that this could all become a dream, or better yet, a cinematic reverie, a show to watch to pass the time. I had more stages to work through, more self-help, self-hate, more memories slipping into my mouth mid-sentence to choke me. Real life doesn't ask that twists be soon followed by curtains and doesn't offer saviors with shields by default. But real life demands no formulaic construction, and there is no script to flip. On the other side of any plot twist that comes my way, I might find—what? I make no predictions. I'll know the answer when I see it.

A Cascade Autobiography

PART 12

My long hair took so long to grow, but once it reached my waist, it was not enough. Any white girl could achieve the same. I studied the other girls' tulip-full hips gesturing toward trim waists that shamed my midsection, which began to pad itself when I hit puberty, and after hearing the other girls complain about thigh fat I had no sense of, I seized upon my mother's reassurance that none of the women in her side of my family had waists. This was a stock shape, passed down from family members so far back they could actually be called *ancestors*. My mother said that when she went to college, in her big state of Washington but far from home, she saw other people with shapes like hers and knew they had to be Indian. I would look at the old photo in our hallway of the stunning and sturdy Abbie and Mary and know I had come out of them. I waited with anticipation until I might come into my inheritance.

In college, I fell for an Indian boy. Nelson was the most beautiful Indian I had ever seen. I wanted to have his quarter-Navajo babies. I wanted to colonize his brown body.

The last time I saw him, the summer before my junior year of college, on the last night of our internship program for Native students, I spooned between him and our friend Ian in a dorm bed, listening to Johnny Cash, breathing on Ian's neck while Nelson breathed on my neck. They didn't try anything. This made them the best guys in the world. We passed out together.

Ian leaned back, stuck his blonde curls into my face, and said, "Lemme in the middle so we can make an Oreo." We shifted. Nelson, one-half Navajo, was browner than I'd be if you baked me. Ian was one-sixty-fourth Cherokee and blonde. My skin spent the summer sunburned while the Navajos' skin turned browner and browner. We all spent the summer whispering about blood quanta as though these fractions were as gossip-worthy as our roommates' boning schedules. All of us worked for the executive branch of the federal government and lived in American University dorms. Nelson and I worked for Agriculture, Ian for Commerce. Nelson would visit me for lunch and sometimes stayed for hours. One day, a Navajo mentor sat down with me and told me to marry Nelson and have children, because I needed to get the quantum up in my bloodline, and Nelson's family was very important because his uncle owned all the Burger Kings on Navajo Nation.

"Don't get a nosebleed," the other kids would tell the white Indians, "or you'll lose your Indian blood."

I shared a dorm with two Navajo girls, Angela and Joanne. Angela didn't believe that Indians who weren't brown-looking should be allowed to be Indians unless they did something to prove themselves, because the culture just couldn't get carried down the generations by Indian blood so thin. My enrollment was not proof enough. My gallbladder disease, described by my Navajo boss as "the Indian curse," was not proof enough. One day I came back to my dorm after work to find the papers and books on my desk replaced by a line of tools used to curl and straighten hair. A week later, Angela took over my bed. By the end of the summer, she was sharing it with Victor, a guy from another summer program. When someone in our program once figured he was one of us and asked him his tribe, Victor said, "Mexican."

After my roommates kicked me out, I rode the Metro home from DC to the Maryland suburbs at night after class. My professor and I often rode together. She looked porcelain, WASPish, but she was tribally enrolled and she practiced tribal law. "You have to remember," she told me, "when times get tough, that the distinction is not ethnic. It's not about color. It's political. Your tribe claims you. You're a member of two nations at the same time. Your blood doesn't matter." It remained in my head, a mantra, for years.

So many times after that summer, I called Nelson up late at night from busy basements and bars, telling him I was coming to see him, or telling him to come see me, and telling him I loved him. He always laughed good-naturedly. I couldn't stop calling—God, one-half, that gorgeous quantum.

Actually—

In the first few years since the first bad fuck happened, I had a hard time creating a complete account of that first time. That shouldn't be a surprise. It used to be hard to tell the truth. I teased it out of myself, a necessary process. In the absence of a police report or other record, I began with a faulty memory riddled with holes.[47] Certainly, I have wondered whether the things I've suddenly remembered really happened. But the recollections' sharp, barbed edges suggest that I forgot on purpose.

That first time, with Damian, I know I said no. I know I had told him I wasn't going to have sex with him so soon. But after he was inside me a little, I opened my legs.[48]

---

47 IM conversations with Noah, my longtime internet friend who I'd never actually met, and who had remained my friend through college. From the morning after the rape:
Elissa: oh my god. ok. i hope you dont mind me telling you all this but i have to.
Elissa: i feel like youre the only person i can really tell this to and i hope youll understand
Noah: is this good news?
Noah: or bad?
Elissa: horrible
Elissa: i cant stop crying
Noah: okay
Elissa: ok so last night Damian finally came here
Elissa: and he was all preoccupied cause his computer died and he didnt eat and stuff
Elissa: but then we had naked time and it made him happier. then we went to wawa around 10 so he could eat.
Elissa: and he was just not being affectionate, but i guess i expected that since he didnt have to try to get anything for me for at least a few minutes.
Elissa: then we ate. then i think there was more naked time.
Elissa: i dont really remember.
Elissa: damian insisted on staying overnight even though i didnt want him to
Elissa: i tried to sleep but i couldnt
Elissa: then....augghh...this is just so embarassing
Elissa: i'd never actually had sex before.
Elissa: not with jake, not with anyone. i'd tried but the pain was too much and jake just couldnt bring himself to hurt me.
Elissa: i know but i joke around like im slutty or something but im totally virginal
Elissa: well i finally decided, i have pain every day, theres nothing to fear

48 Elissa: so then i had sex with damian. and it hurt but i felt like i'd accomplished something and i thanked him for breaking my hymen.
Elissa: then he was being pretty nice and affectionate
Elissa: and then eventually he fell asleep
Elissa: oh yeah and he forgot to tell me that the towel i had between my legs to absorb the blood was the semen towel
Elissa: i told him to get the clean one
Elissa: anyway
Noah: the...?
Noah: semen towel?
Elissa: he had used it earlier to mop some up

Of course there was no condom.[49] I did ask for one. I thought he went soft from

---

Noah: oh
Noah: gotcha
Elissa: so, then i couldnt sleep
Elissa: and i worried because jake was going to call in the morning and i didnt want him to hear
damian there or anything
Elissa: i didnt sleep all night
Elissa: as damian slept i would touch his shoulder or something but he would move away
Elissa: finally in the morning i told damian to wake up and i wanted him to leave
Elissa: and he got mad at me
Noah: mad how
Elissa: and i told him nobody seems to care about what i want, which is why he didnt care that i didnt
really want him to sleep over
Elissa: i dunno he was just really sleepily annoyed and saying nothing
Elissa: and i asked him if he knew he moved away from my touch in his sleep
Elissa: and he said, yes, of course
Elissa: and i started crying and he got dressed
Elissa: and he wasnt even going to say goodbye
Elissa: and i said, do you hate me
Elissa: and he just looked at me and finally said, no, but don't have regrets. then he just left.
Noah: I'm sorry
Elissa: a little while ago i called him and he just sounded like he was really mad at me and didnt want
to have anything to do with me
Elissa: and im sad, and im bleeding, and im crying, and i can barely look at my bed which used to be
my favorite thing, and i feel like ive made the biggest mistake ever.
Elissa: and thats it. im sorry for unloading
49   Elissa: wait
Elissa: ok
Elissa: i need a pill
Elissa: i mean
Elissa: ok
Elissa: GOD im stupid
Elissa: ok my fucking god
Noah: it doesnt matter how it sounds, focus on what's important here
Elissa: ok i need to go get it.
Elissa: but will it be on my insurance or something?
Noah: i dont know
Noah: aks
Elissa: ok
Noah: ask*
Elissa: oh my god
Elissa: this is so bad
Noah: if you'd rather i can call the health center here and descirbe the situation
Elissa: well
Elissa: um
Elissa: i actually did something totally irresponsible...he didnt have a condom on
Noah: ooooookay
Elissa: it kind of just occurred to me
Noah: well
Elissa: but he wasnt even close to ejaculation
Noah: then there is no need to ask anything
Elissa: but, you know
Noah: go
Noah: go now
Elissa: oh my god im so stupid
Elissa: ok

my screams; later, I learned that he went soft every time he fucked. I remember how he pulled out, like a serrated knife, and then beat off, looking at the ceiling, rolling his eyes in shame. Then he was hard again and there was no trace of shame on his face.

He had started the act and I was going to make him see it through. He had begun to push—I was dry, it hurt worse than anything ever had, like I already said, I got that part right—and I thought, if I am going to have to live with this event for the rest of my life, I am at least going to get this one thing out of it: experience. I would never have to be a virgin again.

I had a lot of time and space to think, with everything happening so far away from my brain. I memorized the way the room looked, how he looked, the rub of my comforter, the cold air from the window, the distance of my arm from the wall he had punched earlier that evening. I could roll my head back and look out the window. I lived in the corner, fourth floor, and all the other windows were so close, but nobody knew what I was doing. Even though I wasn't doing much of anything, I felt that I was guilty of something.

I had tried to have sex once before, with Jake, but I was unusually tight, as my doctor had told me; I couldn't even have pap smears. Jake, my *lovey*, as we called each other in high school, couldn't bear to hurt me. I thought this could be my life: anyone I would love enough to give it up to would love me too much to break me. And so I thought that the solution had found me; on top of me was someone who cared so little

---

Noah: and buy the damn pill
Noah: it doesnt matter if its on insurance
Elissa: ok
Elissa: im going
Elissa: youre right
Elissa: bye bye
Noah: bye
Noah: get a recipt if possible!
Elissa: ok
Elissa: bye
Noah: damian should pay half of it
Elissa: i know
Elissa: god
Elissa: why did i let him do that
Noah: but ok, go
Elissa: ok
Elissa: bye
Elissa: oh btw
Noah: ill be here when you get back

about me that he'd ignore my "no," he cared so little that he could even enjoy himself while my tissue tore around him.

"I'm not gonna lie," he said later, "That felt really good."

I said, "I'm glad it was you."[50]

---

50   Noah: how do you feel
Elissa: pretty horrible
Elissa: i'm just not sure of whether to hate damian
Noah: well i wouldnt feel too kindly toward him right now
Noah: gave you a scare
Elissa: i definitely dont feel kindly
Elissa: yeah
Elissa: but actually the nurse said the chance was very very low even without the morning after pill
Elissa: i mean...he could just be ignorant, not careless
Elissa: i dont know
Elissa: hes a bitch
Elissa: fuck damian
Noah: he didnt know theere was a low chance
Noah: for all he knew, there was a high chance
Elissa: well i sort of had a hunch
Elissa: i mean, without ejaculating theres not much goin on
Noah: that's not sure enough
Elissa: thats true
Elissa: i should be mad at him. it is right to be.
Elissa: he took advantage of me. even if he didnt get off right then the point was so he could in the future.
Elissa: im so mad at him
Elissa: when i go down there ill give him his fucking dvd back and have done with him.
Noah: i support that plan 100%
Elissa: great
Elissa: but of course its not that simple
Elissa: actually
Elissa: i just remembered something.
Noah: and you need to not let people take advantage of you.
Elissa: ok. this is going to sound really bad.
Noah: they do that you know.
Elissa: they sure do
Noah: what's bad
Elissa: ok
Elissa: like 5 minutes before it happened i was trying to sleep
Noah: spur of the moment
Elissa: and i was thinking, you know, we've had a lot of naked time together but i dont think anything can happen with this guy because theres a lot about him im not into.
Noah: i see
Noah: well now there's one more thing.
Elissa: and then it happened. and as it happened i was thinking, im glad it's him because he'll break my hymen and then i wont have to have an embarassment happen with someone i actually like. imagine that happening. how horrible.
Noah: okay now i dont agree with that at all
Noah: i mean well
Noah: i kind of do
Noah: but its leaving a lot out
Elissa: i know
Elissa: but...ive sort of always felt this way

I couldn't sleep all night, so I wrote. Back then, I wrote one-page stories in which everything of importance could be said in fewer than five hundred words.

THE VIRGIN WHITE

It is 6 a.m. and the white-on-white stripes on the comforter are all fucked up, twisted, dipping low across your back into the valley spanning the human-sized space between us and back up my soft kidney flesh crossing the continental divide of my knobby spine.

You mumble in your sleep, and point to the ceiling, and turn.

I'm twenty, so of course it's proper to put out on the third date.

I've been trying to sleep for an hour. I crawl across the bed, head down, avoiding your legs like thick roots of trees growing across the sheets. Nakedness: I wrap myself in a black sheet for the voyage across the bedroom.

Faintly, vaguely, I remember you saying you'd be there to hold me when it was all over. You mumble in your sleep, sounds like "serve the ovary," and turn. In the bathroom I wipe with white. The blood is already brown.

At ten I handed Damian his clothes and told him to leave. He didn't say a word. Later, I called him, crying, to apologize. He refused to accept.

My friend talked me into going to the campus health center.[51] I bled all day. I thought I could possibly use a tampon now that I was broken, so I tried, and it worked, and I thought, look at all the good that's come out of this. Of course I wanted this.[52]

Noah: and the important thing thats being left out is that if it's a good person, he'll care about you enough that there's nothing to be embarrased about
Elissa: now thats true.
Noah: i dont know, it always seemed something of a mystery to me of why a person would have sex with someone who cared so little that...that...i dont know. like - like caring about someone enough that no embarassing situation would come between you, that should be a prerequisite.
Elissa: thats true
Elissa: but, i dont know, things with damian have been really weird
Elissa: i mean, i wasnt self conscious naked because i just didnt give a crap perhaps
Elissa: i dont know
Elissa: i guess i just never felt like what i had to offer was sacred

51   In United States law, an outcry witness is the person who first hears an allegation of abuse by a child or another victim of abuse or sexual crime. The witness is legally obligated to report the abuse, and may be called upon during the trial proceedings

52   Elissa: can i pretend i never had sex?
Noah: hm
Noah: to whom
Elissa: can i just repress it?
Noah: and for how long
Elissa: to myself

And it's true, I let him fuck me four more times before he sent me a bunch of text messages calling me a slut because I found a boyfriend to protect me.

Damian taught me how to use a lighter. I wasn't good at it because the skin on my thumb was too raw. Now I have a little callus there. I wish I were as tough as that skin.[53]

My friend Joe lived upstairs. I begged him to come down and help me change my sheets, exchange the black for the floral. I told him I couldn't do it on my own, and he said he did it on his own all the time and I had to learn, but I reminded him that I lugged my laser printer upstairs for him so he had to do this for me. The laser printer, the black sheets: I still use them, relics from my old life, and it's hard to imagine that they really exist.

Other relics: Damian's blog, which still exists, intact. Choice excerpts:

> March 2005
> **Home Team vs. Elissa** - Early lead was blown just as things started to get going well. She didn't understand that I actually did care about her. Even though there were quite intimate occasions, she was ok with moving on to someone new. That's ok, I would have been settling.
> **Result:** Loss
>
> June 2005

Elissa: forever
Noah: eh i wouldnt advise it.
Elissa: i dont know what else to do
Noah: make peace with it
Elissa: i feel like it was such a mistake but i cant figure out why
Elissa: i mean, it seems that perhaps i only think it's a big deal because everyone else does
Elissa: i am bleedin like a motherfucker
53 Noah: you need to take care of yourself
Elissa: no
Noah: YES
Elissa: i need to let me waste away
Noah: no
Noah: dont
Noah: i woudl not appreciate that
Elissa: i do
Noah: that woud be cruel
Elissa: why
Noah: because it would break my heart
Elissa: why
Elissa: i feel like i dont deserve to be vibrant anymore
Noah: because i care about you, i dont want you to be hurt.
Elissa: i did something stupid and betrayed myself

Can't teach an old dog new tricks? What is it they say? Once a slut always a slut?

Elissa's reply: Please stop referring to so many girls as sluts. Drop your double-standard.

Damian: i can double standard all i want. girls are sluts. period.

Elissa: So it's not okay for girls to move on/change their minds/whatever, but guys can insist on proudly recounting their every kiss, relationship, etc., can keep a running tally of each conquest . . . ? Go ahead and set your double standard. You won't have success. Soon you'll realize that your attitude toward women needs to be revamped.

Damian: my attitude towards women has worked for 10,000 years.

For several years, I was drawn to Damian's Facebook page and blog. Something drove me to make sure he still existed. One day, I briefly ran into trouble finding him on Facebook and panicked, worrying that I had lost my only tangible evidence of the very real horror at which I was still chipping away. I found his profile, found his blog, and my world was once again in order. The new developments in his life and the women in it simultaneously repulsed me and strengthened my understanding of the dark force I had encountered:

> January 2009
>
> It just makes me want to fuck her. Vengefully. But she won't have that. And now that I know, neither will I, truthfully.
>
> You know I like my girls a little bit older.
>
> My entire view of life and love and fidelity has been systematically devastated since the first time I had carnal knowledge of a girl. And. I. Can't. Deal.

Good thing for relics. Working with my memory has been a trying process, but it has been helpful to access the rich nuggets residing on my hard drive, at least as a completely intact and un-degraded record of my translation of feelings to text at the time of expression. Accessing the data is like seeing my life on tape. I wrote the following story for my fiction class when I was still getting fucked by Damian. My teacher was concerned and talked to me after class. I assured her that it was fiction, and it was: the kind that never really happened, exactly, but is completely true in every way.

THROUGH THE WINDOW

Baby says, I hate these goddamn sports bras, the kind with no hooks in the back, just solid fabric. I shrug. I tell him underwire hurts my tits this time of the month, when they're all tender, when I'm all fertile.

Shut up, baby says, smiling and kissing my ear. He loves me. When we're in my apartment I forget all the stupid shit in my life. I forget the doctor—no, I mean the nurse—no, actually, she was a nurse practitioner—earlier today, telling me she thought this boy may have taken advantage of me because if he cared he would have worn a condom.

But now I know, the bitch just didn't understand.

My baby pulls it gentle over my head and tries to find a sexy way to slide off my pants, but like always, they get caught up in my feet, and they end up bunched around one leg.

I reciprocate. I move his hand off my belly so I can tug off his shirt. He likes me looking like a mammal, like something that can give birth, so he likes my belly, likes how it swells just a little, the shape of a dish that's not a plate, but not a bowl either.

I forget to mention to him that I haven't eaten in three days. I don't say that looking at food makes me want to vomit.

Baby's big hands guide my hips and my shins and my back into position, the position he wants me in, different tonight just like always.

I also forgot to tell him about going to the doctor. I figure if he knows I took the morning-after pill, he'll think I'm a little pussy.

The condoms are all the way across the room, probably, in the dresser, and it's not like I can go get one. I hope that the morning-after pill works for days. I have to remember to move the Trojans closer to the bed.

The nurse thought my loss of appetite was connected to stress and anxiety. She thought this was a problematic sexual situation.

The blinds fall in parallel diagonals against the window. Little slices of streetlight cut across my baby's chest, cast yellow sheen over each hair.

Baby orders, now scoot forward. Put your rack up on the windowsill. Ah, that's a good girl. My nipples squint at the coldness of the whitewashed wood.

When I'm with him, I can put it all out of my head. All the trash talk about him and me coming from everyone looking in at us.

Because when baby smiles, I feel okay. When baby's eyes roll to the ceiling, I forget the nurse's face.

He crawls up my back and rubs against my fleshy ass, my curdled cellulite skin.

"Now open the blinds."

He loves me. I peer out at the courtyard, at the apartment buildings across the way, the yellow windows with shapes moving inside. I think of the people who see me like this, my nubby body splayed in the window like a framed portrait, some deranged nude, sometimes sucking dick and liking it, sometimes creamed all over front and back, sometimes getting it sideways frontways backways. I feel my face break into hotness, red like private flesh.

I feel him beaming, that angelic smile, those squinting eyes.

You don't want to? He asks, and his face looks sad. He knows I don't.

But, baby, I will.

Another flash piece, written months after the event, after the blog entry about sluts:

MAKEOVER

The third girl I ever slept with just walked by my window. She's dressing up nice now, low heels and a skirt that's the right length for them. Her eye makeup is dark and her lips are puckered mauve.

She ended it with me three months ago. I wasn't sorry; my bad for getting involved with a slut. Once a slut, always a slut.

The blister on the back of her right heel makes her drag her foot, just a little.

I heard she's a porn fiend now, but she won't talk about it with anyone. She likes the girls with tits nothing like hers, big saline things, lots of cleavage. She fast-forwards when the girls' faces get creamed on. That's what I hear, anyway.

People have been talking. She doesn't give head anymore, she won't let anyone fuck her from behind. Whatever, my hands are clean. She didn't press charges because she always said yes. I might call her and leave her a message. We could watch porn together.

After the work my brain did to deny the ordeal, I had to actively put the facts back together if I was to resolve anything at all. Reading through the stories evoked the dread. Late-night Facebook-stalking him, however ill-advised, reminded me that he was no imaginary friend. As I looked through his posted photos and remembered his lips and fists, I knew what had happened: I tried so hard to forget it, called it consensual a thousand times, but here it was, feeling like rotting meat in my stomach, knots in my back, and just like that, the chills I felt skittering up my spine were reminiscent of the Jersey cold I felt in December 2004 when I had long outdoor phone conversations with him, searching for cell reception outside my parents' house, or the chill of a two-jacket night in Maryland, smelling a little like the beer on his breath from his tries to get warm, when he'd come to me in the night, demanding something. Recalling these details was not pleasurable, but I did not want to forget them. Rape is an important thing. I let it keep its assigned pain, and then I worked to isolate it. After that, I worked to separate it from the rest of my sex life. Two-jacket nights became just fine, blow jobs were do-able, old stories were okay too. With all the memories in place, one by one, I made sure they only hurt me when I let them. Little by little, the nausea at the thought of it dissipated.

Perhaps true closure can't come—I have no plans to look the rapist in the face and tell him he's a sad little man. I can't seek justice through the legal system, and when the news stories speak of "closure," that's the only platter on which it's served. But I don't need to seal off the ordeal into a closed compartment—I moved through it. The wreckage of my early twenties looked like a battlefield littered with partners' bodies, and for years, I wielded my anger like a sword, making my hate count, keeping the gash open. With the rapist out of my world, I carried out those duels against myself, a poor sparring partner, beaten-down and humbled. In time, though, my sword became one like that of the archangels, their leftover armaments from the war in heaven. I expelled the demon. I carry the fiery sword. In battle, catcalled on a two-jacket night or urged upstairs after a date that needs to end, I will wrap my great wings around my brilliant body, clutch my celestial hilt, and quietly protect what's mine.

A Cascade Autobiography

PART 13

Until college, I lived in the same house in New Jersey my whole life. My white next-door neighbor erected a tipi in his front yard during some summers, and so I grew up believing that it was customary for white Protestants to raise tipis during the summer. Meanwhile, my family spent the sweltering, air-conditioning-free days in our cool basement, dug out of the side of a hill like an ancient earth lodge. The neighbor man gave us a painting of an Indian Warrior on black velvet. My mom hung it up in the living room, and he said he appreciated the spot she chose because he could look right into our window and see it any time he wanted. We would sit at his kitchen table and nod while he would bring out his beadwork and leatherwork for us to admire. I think I remember seeing him wearing a fringed suede vest over his tanned, naked chest, but my memory might be reaching too far to invent that detail. His daughter used to put me up on their gray-shingled doghouse and spank my bare ass. That, I know. I didn't say anything. She was a year older than me, so I remained still and quiet while she spanked me. Bad habits start young.

In third grade, the principal of my school asked me in front of the whole class, as we peered over our peanut-butter-and-cardboard pueblos, whether I preferred to be called "Indian" or "Native American." When I was in college, a woman from the Office of Multi-Ethnic Student Education insisted I help plan a powwow, because that is traditional Native American knowledge. She wanted me to greet the crowd in my Native language, so I tried to figure out what language that would be and then combed the internet for help saying "Hello, friends" in Chinook Jargon. She told me to wear regalia, and when I said I didn't have any, she said she'd rent me some. I thought about printing a T-shirt resembling those old "THIS IS MY COSTUME" shirts that would read, "THIS IS MY REGALIA." Steal that idea and I'll hunt you down and scalp you.

Many Famous People Suffer
from Bipolar Disorder

THE DEPRESSIVE EPISODE EXEMPLIFIED BY THE LIFE OF KURT COBAIN

When I was fourteen, I loved Kurt and I hated him. Bipolar relationships often inspire such feelings. But Kurt had been dead for four years when I loved and hated him. He could do nothing new to impress or repulse me, but I could sift through the discussion forum threads and fan pages. At fourteen, I had eyeliner and attitude: that's thought of as a phase. Nobody knew I would talk to Kurt's ghost, but they knew something was up, and I had to visit with the guidance counselor once a week. She would try to convince me not to kill myself, and I would try to convince her that I really, really wasn't going to. I wasn't as stupid and selfish as my hero.

I wanted to move to Seattle because it seemed as good a place as any to be blue. Thirteen years after Kurt died, I moved. What did I expect to find? Ghosts thrive here, but they never talk to me. At the end of my first Seattle late-autumn, at Linda's Tavern, the bar where Kurt was last seen alive, a friend of a friend kept refilling my pint glass and resting his hand on my thigh. Moving through the compartments of the bar, Kurt must have been noticed, much more visible than I. The friend of a friend sexually assaulted me that night. I left my body when I flattened my back against the couch and the friend tried to get inside me. No ghosts passed through the room, no guardian angels. I was all by myself, without Kurt's ghost watching over me the way at fourteen I dreamed he would. That's what happens when someone kills himself: he's gone. So I fell back into my body and took care of myself. No one else can.

I wished he'd hovered near me guardian angel-style that night at Linda's, or hugged me as I waited for a cab the next morning. Ghosts are not real. And if Kurt were a ghost now, he'd never visit me.

THE PATIENT MAY FEEL SAD, BLUE, OR "DOWN IN THE DUMPS."

For so long, Kurt could only see drizzle and fog, the pale hair that hid his chlorine eyes, only moved through his world of callused fingers, shredded jeans, evergreen trees. Some say the weather in Washington makes people want to die, but his problem was the storm in his stomach, the misfiring lightning in his head. Sadness isn't the word.

Maybe oversaturated blood churning, maybe brain bleeding, eye knives, psychic head wound, asbestos innards, polluted Puget Sound pooling in his bed.

Being famous, creative, and rich looks easy, but that isn't true: everyone knows this. Kurt's bipolar brain was cloudy, blooming with blue-green algae, rich with phosphorous, with fish corpses floating to the surface. People say celebrity is a monster, or intelligence is; they say it makes you feel things you shouldn't feel, know things like some oracle. Not true. The disorder killed Kurt: genes, circuitry, abnormal anatomy, and then the kindling effect, when every episode added to the burning down of the house in his head. A person doesn't have to be famous or brilliant to be fucked up. She can be completely insignificant: twenty-four with useless degrees from respected universities, thirty-nine pairs of sneakers, no substance abuse problems, and very few Google search results.

Before the fame hit, and after, Kurt was ill. Every high and low was tethered to his spine when he tried to die in Rome, and the pain rocking the tender spine surrounded by stony vertebrae pinned him to a plan. A few weeks later, in sunny L.A., he hatched a new plan, climbed a six-foot fence that was keeping him in rehab, and went back home to die.

IN CLINICALLY DEPRESSED PATIENTS, OCCASIONS FOR CELEBRATION OFTEN HAVE LITTLE INFLUENCE OVER DARK MOODS.

Bipolar opposites attract. Courtney was Nyquil-smooth, volatile, could make him sick to his stomach or incapacitated with desire. Torn lace, velveteen torso, snapped cords, skin under her nails. Replaced codeine, he said, as the only thing that could save him. When things went well, salvation looked like twin needles, Waikiki wedding photos of mismatched blonde hair, a kidney bean on a sonogram. Even when things went bad, she brought him back from overdose in two minutes flat. Of course it was co-dependence. Still, Kurt didn't have to destroy himself alone the way I did, twisting the butterfly knife's tip into my arm, then wiping spots of blood on black sheets where it would disappear, hoping that someone would notice the wound later. Then anxiety pills. Company would have been kind of nice.

IN BIPOLAR PATIENTS, MANIC EPISODES MAY BE TRIGGERED BY SCHEDULE CHANGES.

A living legend in plaid, he represented an apathetic generation while his feelings were so real they had fingernails. Touring hurt, threw kindling on the fire. The hoards of live, steaming bodies could tip him into mania. Spray paint and stones, screams born from vocal cords living on cough syrup, promises of salvation bleeding in his stomach. Every evening, he looked out over thousands of people who thought they knew him. The loping bass held the rhythm of his pulse, a guitar was plugged into his aorta. When hubris overwhelmed him, his brow contracted, his knees quaked, and his throat swallowed itself and became silent.

MANY WHO SUFFER FROM DEPRESSION AND BIPOLAR DISORDER SELF-MEDICATE WITH STREET DRUGS AND ALCOHOL.

The heroin addiction was on purpose, he said. His stomach killed. By 1992 he really did seem to be dying. In photo shoots, every shot captured his last breath. The camera's blinking eye caught him sleeping, his face softened into the clay features of a four-year-old boy. He was becoming an embryo, melon stomach melting into sandy brown bays. A river was born at the summit of his syringe, and through water he saw his arms around the stout chest of a tree, splattered Easter eggs at his feet. A child ran from him, could have been his brother, his father. Did he have either? He thought that was the problem until he slipped far enough under to converse with his misfiring synapses. Then a flashbulb reminded him that he needed to tell the world that he was still breathing. Under gray stars his sonogram eyes saw the sun turn blue, and he awoke.

A FAILED SUICIDE ATTEMPT BY DRUG OVERDOSE MAY OFTEN BE A "CRY FOR HELP."

On tour in 1994, his throat and lungs decided to stop what was happening. No more screaming. He went to Rome to fix the bronchitis and laryngitis. Courtney had a bottle of fresh pills. In a water-soaked, warped world, he slept in a spoon, was fed by his glands. Rohypnol x 50, they said, blue-tinted champagne. When I read about it, long after he had successfully offed himself, I needed to know where to get these things, roofies and champagne. He was so dead that he had nothing to do with me. He was not so dead that I couldn't imagine the long side of his delicate body making a silhouette in the mattress. A host of sacred questions—are you there? they asked. Comatose, no movable tongue for hours, until his sleeping hand remembered to clutch.

THE DEPRESSED PERSON WILL OFTEN WITHDRAW FROM NORMAL SOCIAL ACTIVITY.

He ruined his tiny family. Ruined the band. Ruined a generation, somehow. Oh, the guilt. As the spokesman for a generation, all he had to do was say thirty words to the camera. Word choice was not important. Sunglasses were key. His yellow hair dripped from jaundiced skin. He spoke through glacial teeth and observed with deep-set eyes that burrowed deep into his brain. The interviewer's owl glare forced confessions. Kurt said something about rock music while he made plans to die, and his insides were bloated with guilt drawn from lakes older than the moon.

BEHAVIORAL INDICATORS OF A SUICIDE ATTEMPT INCLUDE:
He acquired a weapon. He hoarded heroin and Valium. He put his affairs in order. He took Courtney out of his will, they say. Everyone knew this was coming. The six-foot fence surrounding the Exodus Recovery Center could not keep him from this. He got on a plane, got off a plane, locked himself in his Lake Washington Boulevard house. He mended no grievances, left them in order. Then, as I might have done fourteen years later if I had the means, a rotten evening, and a less robust drug regimen to keep me afloat, he shot heroin into his bloodstream and bullets into his face.

SUICIDE IS A RESULT OF THE LEVEL OF PAIN EXCEEDING THE RESOURCES FOR DEALING WITH PAIN.
When he looked down the long eye sockets of his shotgun, he blinked and saw the heart he swallowed, a memory, lost in his throat. Selfishness let him off the hook. When he allowed himself to die, he left the tiny pinpricks to explain what he could not.

SUICIDE LEAVES LASTING IMPRINTS ON THE FRIENDS, FAMILY, AND LOVED ONES LEFT BEHIND.
I loved Kurt so much that from age fourteen to seventeen, I retreated into an online message board dedicated to the band. Thousands of us were not about to forget him. We maintained his life in electronic form the way parents might seal off the bedroom of a dead child. We still wore Chucks and Docs and flannel. I wore my dad's flannel shirts in twos to ward off the New Jersey cold. Every morning of my first high school winter, I checked the Seattle weather online. Seattle seemed exciting and dark and damp and full of danger. People did hard drugs there. People felt as shitty as I did.

I grew up a little, forgot about Kurt, and moved to Seattle anyway. People do not feel as shitty as I do. The city's flannel-soft focus has sharpened, its film has lifted, and now I live in a city of Lululemon-clad yoga moms and hipster girls in one-of-a-kind dresses that baffle me in their ability to look like uniforms. Still, even though I thought Kurt was kind of a dick, he at least wrote some very good songs, and so on my Monday-Tuesday karaoke nights, I've recently started letting his ghost nest in my throat. The night I sang "Smells Like Teen Spirit," I brought earth where Tori Amos, in her cover version, had brought air. I gouged valleys where Kurt had scratched with claws.

I had been living in Seattle for a year and a half before I finally got around to looking up his last address. The house where Kurt died is up above the road, right off Lake Washington. Next door is a park where fans still gather every year on April fifth, where "Fuck you you fucking ass hole RIP" is written on a bench in Sharpie. My GPS led me to this spot, the road to which appeared as a double-bended pink snake on the screen, a terrifying—but not even accurate—representation of the two joints in the downward slope of Lake Washington Boulevard. The road parts tall trees which, this time of year, are as bare and skinny as Kurt's forearms.

I do not miss him. I'm all grown up now, being sad is uncool, and instead of medicating with heroin, I medicate with antipsychotics and antidepressants the FDA approved ten years after Kurt's death. I cannot get better if rock-bottom looks appealing, and I'm not fourteen anymore, so the appeal is gone.

Pearl Jam still makes albums, though I thought their 2006 self-titled album with an avocado on the cover was an unlistenable all-time low, and I am unofficially no longer a fan. Axl Rose is still an asshole. Dave Grohl, bearded, looks like a grown-up. In 2008, Kurt's daughter Frances Bean had a $300,000 suicide-themed sweet sixteen party, but she still seemed saner than her parents. Courtney has dabbled in eating disorders and committed to crazy. In 2002, a compilation of facsimile pages from Kurt's journals were published, and now we all know him so well it's like he's still alive.

The house where Kurt died by shotgun blast does not look like the house of a dead rock star. The neighborhood is as scenic as Warren County, New Jersey, more so than any part of Seattle I've seen, with its guardrails, tree cover, and lack of any light but that which I supplied. I could see why he came here to die. He might have thought that no person who cared about him would hear a shot and no one would ever find him. I realized then that Kurt wasn't crying for help when he downed fifty roofies in Rome. He was working on killing himself the way I work on quitting smoking: with every attempt, you get closer to the real thing.

The morning after my pilgrimage, I read a blog post about the return of grunge fashion. Mary-Kate Olsen walked around New York in a shapeless flannel shirt. Ripped jeans will come back any day now, but mine haven't fit since I was under-medicated and underweight. I don't really miss them. I went to my closet, pulled out my eight-eye Docs, and went out to buy a pack of Parliaments. Everything old is new again.

THE MANIC EPISODE EXEMPLIFIED BY THE LIFE OF BRITNEY SPEARS

Now they're saying she's not just crazy, not just unstable, but sick. They're talking about diagnosis and treatment. They're talking about drug therapy. The conventional wisdom says that depression turns inward, mania outward; it's heroin binges versus million-dollar shopping sprees, suicide versus a comeback.

Kurt's depression was syrupy, wearing the soft gray flannel of the early nineties. Britney ushered in oversaturated MTV hues, gleaming vinyl, and sparkly skin. Britney was featured on *The New Mickey Mouse Club* at the time of Kurt's suicide, not yet wearing shorts with "Baby" spelled out in rhinestones across the ass, not yet pissing off the American Family Association, and not yet appearing bloated and tear-streaked in photos displayed at newsstands from Kentwood, Louisiana to Seattle.

EXCESSIVE HAPPINESS, HOPEFULNESS, AND EXCITEMENT MAY BE SIGNS OF A MANIC EPISODE.
It is dangerous to be too hopeful. Excitement is inadvisable. Check yourself. Hope is the thing that comes before the very fucking scary thing.

THE PERSON FEELS THAT NOTHING CAN PREVENT HIM OR HER FROM ACCOMPLISHING ANY TASK.
In 1998, the cutie could dance and had a somewhat decent voice. At seventeen, she had a fleet of people who were going to make her a star. First, she had to morph from a child into a brand. I saw her on TV in a schoolgirl outfit more often than I saw my friends in person. I would change the channel, looking for KoRn, every fucking time that stupid video came on. I was depressed and I didn't want to see that happy shit. Though I hoped she would disappear forever, things were looking up for the young star. When was someone going to whisper to Britney that something wasn't right here?

THE PATIENT MAY MAKE REPEATED CALLS TO 900 SEX NUMBERS. THIS, UNFORTUNATELY, IS ANOTHER SYMPTOM OF BIPOLAR HYPERSEXUALITY.
A Rolling Stone review of *Oops!... I Did It Again* reads, "Britney's demand for satisfaction is complex, fierce and downright scary." Britney, though, didn't write any of the songs, except for a contribution to the track "Dear Diary." I think of her posed for hours, bearing her sexy-face, working toward the perfect shot by remaining very still. There is a difference between wanting to fuck and having the whole world wanting to fuck you.

MANIA CAN CAUSE DISASTROUS SPENDING SPREES. THE PATIENT'S CARD OR CHECKBOOK MAY NEED TO BE CONFISCATED.

As her court-appointed conservator, Britney's estranged father played Daddy again. The court classified her as an adult child in need of financial—and general—supervision. Soon I fear that I am going to need a conservatorship, after I spend all my money on MAC eyeshadow, Ralph Lauren sundresses, Nikes, computer peripherals, cocktails, antipsychotics, various kinds of body waxing kits, books, red wine (for the antioxidants), and printer paper, and have to give up my life in Seattle to move back into my parents' house in New Jersey, where I will have nothing to spend money on.

SOME PEOPLE WITH BIPOLAR DISORDER BECOME PSYCHOTIC, HEARING THINGS THAT AREN'T THERE. THEY MAY HOLD ONTO FALSE BELIEFS, AND CANNOT BE SWAYED FROM THEM.

That grainy picture of Britney in the stylist's chair, wrapped in a bib, with half her grody black hair shaved off, has become an icon of rotted fame. What the fuck was that girl thinking?

I imagine she said, "Shave my fucking head. Do it." The stylist said no. "My extensions are too tight." Stylist said, "No, come back when you think it over." Britney grabbed the buzzer and did it herself.

Why did she do it? Sometimes you just have to cut your hair. A few days after I was sexually assaulted, I stopped into a barbershop on the way to my car, and said, "Cut my hair short, like a boy's." He did, and while it grew back into something decently feminine, I recovered.

"People shave their heads every day," Britney said in 2009, from a place of wise remove.

Long, lustrous hair is the mark of a healthy individual, ready to bear young. Freudians consider long hair to represent the id and aggression, so they associate cutting long hair with killing sexuality. Look at Samson, whose strength relied on the length of his hair. For many Indian tribes, cutting hair symbolizes a severance from the past, or mourning. Perhaps the most accurate explanation of Britney's actions, though, is that the authorities who are trying to snatch your babies away can't hair test you for past drug use when you're hairless. The salon owner speculated that maybe Spears is on the cutting edge of a new trend.

MANIC EPISODES OFTEN CAUSE DELUSIONS OF GRANDEUR. IN SOME INSTANCES, PATIENTS SEE THEMSELVES AS HAVING SUPERHUMAN SKILLS AND POWERS—EVEN CONSIDER THEMSELVES TO BE GOD-LIKE.

"Britney Spears" has ended the year as the most-searched term on Yahoo! seven times in total. Her body has been perfect enough that millions of orgasms occurred with her image in mind, or in glossy form, or on a computer screen. Her grandeur—not grandiosity like mine—was no delusion.

Sometimes I'm surprised I'm not dead. I'm even more surprised that she isn't. She must have a deific piece somewhere in that body that has been photographed, jerked off to, asked to dance, stage-lit, and critiqued so many times it barely seems to have ever existed in real, physical form. Maybe I worship her a little. Britney is a bipolar role model: even though she must feel as though every human on earth has seen her melt down, and even though her ex-husband and father control everything that has ever been hers, she sweats to regain it all.

INDIVIDUALS IMAGINE THAT THEY HAVE SPECIAL CONNECTIONS WITH GOD, CELEBRITIES, OR POLITICAL LEADERS.

Who was more godlike in 2000: Britney Spears or Justin Timberlake? Justin is more famous than ever; Britney is infamous. He sings that the old Justin is dead and gone while sources tell *Us* that Britney will always, always, always love him. He was her first love, he was her true love, but now he's singing about his dick in a box while Britney's box is readily available through Google image searches because her lazy thighs have sleepily parted to greet photographers during her careless exits from cars.

THE PERSON BEHAVES IN A RECKLESS OR RISKY MANNER, WHICH MAY BE CHARACTERIZED BY RECKLESS DRIVING, OUTLANDISH SPENDING SPREES, FOOLISH BUSINESS INVESTMENTS, OR OUT-OF-CHARACTER SEXUAL BEHAVIOR.

Tabloid-worthy shit I have never done: drive around with a baby in my lap, appear on the cover of *Harper's Bazaar* naked and hugely pregnant, check into rehab, shave skull on a whim, trash a neighbor's car out of something kind of like rage and kind of like grief, attack a paparazzo's car with an umbrella, hit-and-run without a license or a care, publicly nip slip, perform nearly naked at the MTV Video Music Awards while within fifteen pounds of overweight, go batshit and get strapped to a gurney, get committed to a psych ward under seventy-two-hour suicide watch, lose control of all assets (monetary and otherwise), publicly vadge-flash, or surrender to a second involuntary psych hold within a month of the first.

Still, when *Britney: For the Record* aired on MTV, after we were both spent from our meltdowns, I felt as though, perched in the hot seat, Britney gave the responses I couldn't broadcast from my couch. She looked like an off-brand Barbie in interview moments, and like a pixie in candid moments. The intro text announced, over piano music, that no topic was off limits and no question went unanswered. But not every question was asked. My questions: Are you bipolar? Do you miss Justin? Do you still love him? How is your drug treatment going? What are you on? Are you like me? Kurt wrote in his journal, after learning to navigate megastardom, "The easiest way to advert from the chance of misrepresentation is to use the Question Answer format. It has been proven for years that this is a safe and effective way to report the truth as long as all of the answers are printed in their entirety."

Britney ends by saying, after scenes of throngs of paparazzi surrounding her car, after tearful interviews and tearless ones, after impersonations of her father and make-up artists, after she says she's not a victim of her success and tries to stay positive and hates being placed in categories, after she dances her fucking ass off to get back what she had, after she explains that she married K-Fed because she liked the idea of it (a revelation that socked me in the chest and made my dating life flash before my eyes), and after she says that "people shave their heads all the time"; after all that, she leaves me with this: "I go through life like a karate kid."

That's it: watch your moods. Don't let people see you fluctuate. Don't let yourself run your mouth. Never ever cry, even alone, because your cat or your kettle might tell. Always smile, but don't laugh loudly. Mania is an extravert, but if you need to vent, tell your mattress or maybe your therapist, but put nothing in writing and never tell a friend or coworker how you're really feeling. Downplay any problem or joy. Pay attention to any signs that your life is shitty or excellent, because either is an illusion. Be careful around men, especially ones with big arms or opinions. Stop talking.

I thought I would want to hug Britney after watching *For the Record*, but I didn't feel much at all, besides overwhelmed. Mania is like a nasty bacterial colony, multiplying like crazy if you give it enough nutrients. I don't know how she stays sane. She might not be real. In the "film," as Britney calls it, she is sometimes put-together, sometimes crying, and my heart curls up into a ball as I think of my own days that were so wonderful I didn't believe in gloom, and days so wretched I would lie snow-angel style in my double bed and try to figure out whether the good days had been real.

The "film" was meant to signal the beginning of the Comeback. The glossy mags say Britney's trim, happy, healthy; tabloids say she's starving herself, addicted to exercise, missing the kids, missing Justin, not missing K-Fed, obtaining fistfuls of restraining orders, legally drugged, requesting twice-weekly colonics, applying many varieties of cellulite cream, gearing up for the *Circus* tour, hating her father's permanent rule, sticking with blondness. She has so much work to do. A caller to Seattle's KISS FM responds to the new "Womanizer" single: "She's gross. She's mentally insane. Why would you wanna have sex with her?"

What does the future hold? If Britney is bipolar, I can predict it.

THE BIPOLAR MIXED STATE EXEMPLIFIED BY THE LIFE OF ELISSA WASHUTA

Call it dysphoric mania, agitated depression, or a mixed state: nobody will understand anyway. Mania and depression at once mean the will to die and the motivation to make it happen. This is why mixed states are the most dangerous periods of mood disorders. Tearfulness and racing thoughts happen. So do agitation and guilt, fatigue and morbidity and dread. Walking late at night, trying to get murdered, happens. Trying to explain a bipolar mixed state is like trying to explain the Holy Trinity, three persons in one God: you just have to take it on faith when I tell you that the poles bend, cross, never snapping.

Goes something like this.

DIAGNOSTIC AND STATISTICAL MANUAL OF MENTAL DISORDERS, FOURTH EDITION (DSM-IV)

MIXED EPISODES:

The criteria are met both for a Manic Episode and for a Major Depressive Episode (except for duration) nearly every day during at least a one-week period. The mood disturbance is sufficiently severe to cause marked impairment in occupational functioning or in usual social activities or relationships with others, or to necessitate hospitalization to prevent harm to self or others, or there are psychotic features.

THE DIAGNOSTIC CODES FOR BIPOLAR I DISORDER ARE SELECTED AS FOLLOWS:

1. The first three digits are 296.

2. The fourth digit is 0 if there is a single Manic Episode. For recurrent episodes, the fourth digit is 4 if the current or most recent episode is a Hypomanic Episode or a

Manic Episode, 6 if it is a Mixed Episode, 5 if it is a Major Depressive Episode, and 7 if the current or most recent episode is Unspecified.

3. The fifth digit (except for Bipolar I Disorder, Most Recent Episode Hypomanic, and Bipolar I Disorder, Most Recent Episode Unspecified) indicates the following: 1 for Mild severity, 2 for Moderate severity, 3 for Severe Without Psychotic Features, 4 for Severe With Psychotic Features, 5 for in Partial Remission, 6 for in Full Remission, and 0 if Unspecified. Other specifiers for Bipolar I Disorder cannot be coded. For Bipolar I Disorder, Most Recent Episode Hypomanic, the fifth digit is always 0. For Bipolar Disorder, Most Recent Episode Unspecified, there is no fifth digit.

In recording the name of a diagnosis, terms should be listed in the following order: Bipolar I Disorder, specifiers coded in the fourth digit (e.g., Most Recent Episode Manic), specifiers coded in the fifth digit (e.g., Mild, Severe With Psychotic Features, In Partial Remission), as many specifiers (without codes) as apply to the course of episodes (e.g., With Rapid Cycling); for example, 296.54 Bipolar I Disorder, Most Recent Episode Depressed, Severe With Psychotic Features, With Melancholic Features, With Rapid Cycling.

I am 296.62. My brain—my swirls of dusty glitter, my gray matter wrung like a sponge—are summed up in a five-digit number.

I have this memory from right before I moved to Seattle:

New York makes me mixed as shit. I forget parts, black out sober. I remember other parts like I saw them in indie films. Last time I was in New York, I met up with this Brazilian guy I only knew from hanging out in the city once before. He seemed like a nice person to pal around with for the afternoon. We met up in Times Square, after I got off the train from Jersey and wandered around for an hour. We went to a party in the Village, like they do in books, and then to somewhere more private. He had just finished an internship at an independent film company specializing in low-budget films featuring shock exploitation—graphic sex and violence, gore and nudity. This guy still had the keys to the offices. Upstairs, the toilet wouldn't flush, and he had told me to leave no trace, so I wrapped my tampon in toilet paper and plastic wrapper and put it in my purse. The guy took me into the head honcho's office, undressed, and shoved his dick in my face. The floor might as well have been the gutter. The lights in the office were off, my clothes were on, my mouth open only because something was in it. It all made sense. My place in the world was right here, on my back, with a naked body hovering over me, lit by the street. He didn't come. He didn't insist on fucking me. Would it have been any different if he had? I found a trash can outside. The sky was fully blue by the time I found Jersey.

Defend yourself by staying aware of your surroundings and avoiding venturing out alone. If you are threatened, attract attention. Use your strongest weapons against his weakest targets. Consider a self-defense course, such as Rape Escape, to educate and empower you. The sport, naturally, began as a European martial art, though it's unlikely that your foil will be of any use to you if you are threatened. Taking your pills as scheduled will make relapse less likely, and treating acute episodes will protect your brain. Wear your sunblock.

You are not a victim. You're a survivor. What's the difference? *It wasn't your fault.* Are you sure about that? *You'll soon regain control over your life.* Just like that? *Have you been having nightmares?* Every night of my fucking life. *You're not alone. You're not the first person to go through this.* But I'm the first person to ever be Elissa. *Take care of yourself.* Why? *Denial is a normal response to trauma.* What trauma are we talking about here?

> We always had plenty; our children never cried from hunger, neither were our people in want. . . . Our village was healthy and there was no place in the country possessing such advantages, nor hunting grounds better than those we had in possession. If a prophet had come to our village in those days and told us that the things were to take place which have since come to pass, none of our people would have believed him.
>
> (From *Autobiography of Ma-ka-tai-me-she-kia-kiak, or Black Hawk*, by Black Hawk, War Chief of the Sauk and Fox, 1882)

I am no movie Indian. Not Sonseeahray from the 1950 *Broken Arrow*, Debra Paget in brownface, as though only a white girl can be pretty enough to play Jimmy Stewart's love interest. Not Natalie Wood's portrayal of Debbie in *The Searchers*, white girl abducted by Indians, braids wrapped, fists bearing blond-haired scalps, white girl become a buck. My scalp was taken long ago. Wavy white-girl hair grows where some old Lieutenant cut the flesh away. My blood should buck against my life as a white girl, but it doesn't.

John Wayne needed Debbie to die as long as she was a buck. When he saw the white girl underneath, he saw the light, softened, and carried her home, delivering her to her *real* people in his arms. Sonseeahray, though, needed to die. She and the white scout could not be. One night of bliss was only permitted because Paget's tinted skin, lusory, protected viewers from witnessing real-life miscegenation. Still, Sonseeahray needed to die after one perfect night with Jimmy Stewart, buckskin against cotton on the stream banks. Saved by a white man, both Paget and Woods. Me, never. My Indian blood is so thin that there are no racial implications here: I am a girl who looks to be saved by other people as much as by pills, sneakers, the South Beach Diet. The men silently offer to save me, and then I die slightly.

For luck, I just busted out my three-year-old winter gear from the closet: down puffy jacket all wilted, old fleece-lined knit cap with earflaps dangling braided wool ropes I like to pull. In my puffy coat, smelling stale old smoke on myself reminds me of something. Everything I think I can't say 'cause it'd come out fucking emo, like, if I were to say what I've been thinking all day, every day: I don't know if I can go on like this forever; or, I'm also always thinking, it shouldn't be this hard just to have a brain. Everyone has a brain. This morning down the hall from my office someone had put some no-longer-needed Christmas ornaments out on a bench, with a note: "Free to good home, happy '09." I put a Santa-hatted white clay bear in my pocket for luck. I rub it and my white lighter for luck. I remember three years ago, those frat boys, saying white lighters are bad luck, and I thought, it can't get any worse: I'm bipolar forever.

Goose down keeps poking out of my coat, fluttering around the car, then getting sucked out into Seattle. I got swagga, remember, I got fame. Don't hate the playa. Hate the game.

In the supermarket, I spot a dude I went on some dates with. I met him at jury duty. He was really nice. Down the coffee aisle I go to avoid him. Then I realize that he'll never recognize me like this; I'm an alien. One head of green lettuce is all I need. At home I take two Seroquel, an extra this time, enough to knock out a puma this time, and I cocoon into two down comforters, black and white, just like everything on earth but my thinking, and try to figure out how to pray.

Instead my head leaps and swims. Who would win in a fight, Rambo or Rocky? Rambo or the Russian? Snap, Crackle, or Pop? Marry, Kill, or Fuck—Mariah Carey, Eminem, Dr. Dre? Bill Clinton, the color red, chicken pot pie? Who would win in a fight, my brain or my heart or my stomach? I lose.

Hail, Holy Queen, Mother of Mercy, our life, our sweetness, and our hope. To thee do we cry, poor banished children of Eve. To thee do we send up our sighs, mourning and weeping in this valley of tears. Turn then, O most gracious advocate, thine eyes of mercy toward us, and after this, our exile, show unto us the blessed fruit of thy womb, Jesus. O clement! (pound heart) O loving! (pound heart) O sweet Virgin Mary! (pound heart) Pray for us, O Holy Mother of God, so that we may be made worthy of the promises of Christ.

I am still here; she must be able to hear me.

A mixed state can be defined as the experience of thinking you are the most incredible being alive and knowing that for that you must be pummeled into the earth.

Top things I hear people say about Britney:
- She's crazy.
- She's kind of interesting.
- I feel sorry for her.
- She's faking because she's a media whore.
- She's so gross.
- She's hot, but I wouldn't stick that.
- I don't think about Britney Spears at all.

About Kurt:
- Rock legend. Left a legacy. Voice of a generation.
- What a tortured person. Poor Kurt.
- Selfish. His poor family.
- Do you think he was murdered?

Comments on me:
- I can't believe how well you're dealing with everything you've been through.
- I think all the time about how fucked up you are.
- You've had a tough year, huh?
- I think we're gonna have to change your diagnosis to bipolar.
- Stop being so needy.
- Elissa Washuta has produced an excellent senior honors paper.
- The bitch cries rape against every guy she fucks.

-You have the best tits.

Kurt had a tummy-ache, Britney had a headache, I had a heartache. Go with your gut. It's all in your head. Your heart is in the right place. Is any of this shit real? Motherfucker, this pain is the realest thing I've ever known. My moods cycle faster than my heart beats. I will not fucking put a smile on my face, unless I'm drunk.

Anton Corbijn famously photographed Kurt's shirtless back, covered in Courtney's gouge marks. Kurt flexes his wiry arms, muscles swelling with pride: he just fucked a real animal. She gouged out enough of his flesh that red marks, like the aftermath of a grizzly bear mauling, crisscross his pasty back.

Kurt, well-known for his layering of flannel and jersey necessitated by Seattle's bone-chilling winter dampness, rarely appears so naked in photographs. Corbijn caught him on a special occasion: a moment of sex pride. I know the feeling. I have skipped dabbing concealer over hickeys, thought about shouting out my bedroom window that I'd lost my virginity. I've felt it enough times that I recognize it, now, as a warning sign, the flush of hormones mixed with the justifications and bravado covering gut feelings when something isn't right. They say Kurt took Courtney out of his will, planned for divorce. Good thing there was no Google Image Search back then, because the photo—you can practically see his grin through the back of his head—is all over the search results for "Cobain." Hope becomes so stupid when it's set into digital stone.

INTERVIEWEE

28   I'm neurotic in bed—

29   that's why no one wants to sleep with me

ELISSA

30   Everybody wants to sleep with you

INTERVIEWEE

31   Fuck that.

32   I have all this Harvard LSD

33   Why doesn't anyone wanna sleep with me

ELISSA

34   Everyone in this room

35   wants to sleep with you

36   <LAUGHS>

37   oh the internal review board's

38   not gonna like that

INTERVIEWEE

39   <LAUGHS AWKWARDLY>

40   uhhhhhhh—

41   everyone in this room.

42   does not want to sleep with you

43   <LAUGHS>

ELISSA

44   <loudly> *ohhhhh* (pause = 1.6)

45   next fucking question asshole

Sometimes, I remember college:

There are haters, and they can go fuck themselves. I am sleek and sexy. I don't need help, I need a fucking tan. Some more heels. Check it out, got these sweet patent leather pink ones. Got my mile time down from thirteen minutes to nine on the treadmill this month. Remember when y'all used to think I was weak? Shy and quiet? Now look who's talking. You are nothing and my legs are ten miles long, my bones show. I'm so awesome that getting bigger and smaller is as easy as inhaling and exhaling. Like Britney on the cover of Star: *flabby 140 on the left, svelte 115 on the right. Sleek and sexy: I will kill myself before I get that fat again. Stars—They're Just Like Us!*

> You have taken me prisoner with all my warriors. I am much grieved, for I expected, if I did not defeat you, to hold out much longer, and give you more trouble before I surrendered. . . . I saw my evil day at hand. The sun rose dim on us in the morning, and at night it sunk in a dark cloud, and looked like a ball of fire. That was the last sun that shone on Black Hawk. His heart is dead, and no longer beats quick in his bosom. He is now a prisoner to the white men; they will do with him as they wish. But he can stand torture, and is not afraid of death. He is no coward. Black Hawk is an Indian.
>
> (From Black Hawk's speech of surrender at Prairie du Chien, August 27, 1832)

In the summers, still, I pay for time at tanning salons. Every few days, I climb into the tanning bed, hard glass scented with cleaning solution. Then the bulbs light up, above and below my body. For ten minutes or more, the light burns me. When the bulbs shut off, I climb to the floor, seeing green in the dim room, and emerge brown, with my brain bathed in serotonin. The true sun notices no infidelity: my brownness is flawless. From Seattle white girl, I become Indian princess, but every glance at the skin cancer warning placards by the beds reminds me that my day will come. I'll be expecting it.

SAINT DYMPHNA (also: **DYMPNA, DIMPNA**) was the daughter of a pagan Irish chief and his Christian wife in the seventh century. Dymphna was beautiful and sweet, like her mother, whom she lost when she was fourteen. Her father Damon scoured the world for a suitable and equally beautiful replacement. After the search failed, his advisors pointed out to the chief that his teenage daughter had inherited her mother's looks. Driven mad by grief and mental illness, Damon tried to fuck his daughter. Together with her confessor, the elderly priest St. Gerebernus, the court jester, and his wife, Dymphna fled to Belgium and took refuge at a chapel. But Damon found her. He ordered his soldiers to slay Gerebernus and begged Dymphna to return with him to Ireland. With undaunted courage, she refused him, and he cut off her head in a rage. The holy virgin died on the fifteenth of May, between the years 620 and 640. She is patroness of sleep-walkers, epileptics, princesses, runaways, the mentally ill, and rape victims.

I wanted to take Dymphna as my confirmation saint. I wanted her name in the middle of mine: Elissa Dymphna Marie Washuta. It sounded good, and I didn't know why. At fourteen, I didn't yet know that my brain had started going bad, that I was six years away from rape and a whole world of fucked-up. Dymphna just seemed like the right saint for me. My parents suggested I choose St. Cecilia, patroness of music, instead, so I did. Then Elissa Cecilia Marie Washuta forgot how to pray, and then later, how to ask for help at all.

When I was fourteen and fifteen, I hung out at a Nirvana internet forum from the time I got home from school until bedtime. Boys on the forum posted pictures of Britney because she was a "sexy little heifer" but otherwise a "waste of sperm and eggs." The worst crime was, as Kurt said, faking it. We waited for Britney to pose nude some-where, but it never happened. Those were the days of her schoolgirl outfits and fitted jumpsuits. The boys said they beat their meat imagining dominating that bitch. It was like Kurt said: we can eat fish, because they won't feel anything.

Some people don't believe in bipolar disorder. I think they're just missing the right metaphors. A mixed state is like a foot cramp, one of those urgent, painful ones; not a tempest, which has been said too many times before; maybe jalapeños, the way they hurt my mouth so badly but they taste good; sunburn, while it's happening, the way the skin feels so hot and it stings but the light is all pleasure. A mixed state is Kurt Cobain jerking off onto a camera during a concert in Brazil; Britney's bald-headed attack with an umbrella, a frightening canine sneer, short-shorts that display perfect legs that once wrapped around a thousand backup dancers in as many routines; my hours sitting in a tunnel in a long white wool coat, heels, and sunglasses to block out the dark surroundings and obliterate all light, while I hoped someone would murder me, because I could not go on as a deity in a world of agnostics. My brain wears bedazzled flannel. Bipolar disorder is more real than happiness or sadness because someday we'll know exactly why it happens, know for sure that it's the chemistry or the wiring or structural defects. Emotions are fleeting: a smile on Britney's face means nothing. A pussy shot on the internet is a pussy shot chiseled into the side of a cliff.

What the Internet told me: You have to heal your body if you want to heal your brain. And in order to heal your body, you have to bring each of the seven key systems in your biology back into balance. The steps to balancing these systems are: Optimize Your Nutrition; Balance Your Hormones; Cool Off Inflammation; Fix Your Digestion; Enhance Detoxification; Boost Your Energy Metabolism; Calm Your Mind. Do this and you're straight. Also, reduce your exposure to heavy metals. Also, avoid environmental petrochemicals, electromagnetic radiation exposure (i.e., be careful of that cell phone because it is poisoning your brain), avoid carbs, exercise regularly—oh, also, are your intestines affecting your brain? Did you know that when the lining of your intestinal tract breaks down, your shit leaks into your bloodstream? Better take care of that. Açai. Kombucha. Certain teas. Do not make dairy a part of your life. Fitness bands, Swiss balls, medicine balls, kettle bells, barbells, elliptical trainers, treadmill, rower, lift, pull, tone, tuck, pant, breathe, build muscle, improve metabolism, stamina, overall well-being. Let me once again stress the importance of overall well-being. You need to manage the stressors in your life. Just improve your life. Make an effort. After all, the problem is nothing more than bad thoughts.

> Black Hawk is a true Indian, and disdains to cry like a woman... He
> cares for his nation and the Indians. They will suffer. He laments
> their fate. The white men do not scalp the head; but they do worse—
> they poison the heart; it is not pure with them. His countrymen
> will not be scalped, but they will, in a few years, become like the
> white men, so that you can't trust them. . . . Farewell, my nation!
> Black Hawk tried to save you, and avenge your wrongs. He drank
> the blood of some of the whites. He has been taken prisoner, and his
> plans are stopped. He can do no more. He is near his end. His sun is
> setting, and he will rise no more. Farewell to Black Hawk.
> (From Black Hawk's speech of surrender at Prairie du Chien, August
> 27, 1832)

Giving up the insanity hurts, feels like killing a part of my brain. Sometimes I think about the old, bad things and try to feel the pain again, try to cry. I watch movies and final episodes of TV shows that I know will bring on the tears, just so I'll cry. I remember those fierce days, those times I screamed into the carpet with my mouth open as wide as it would go, or the times my tingling forehead felt like it was about to detach and float up into the night sky. I have beaten my brain like a bad dog. It now submits. I now feel happy when something good happens, and sad when things aren't so good. I only cry when I'm hurt or scared, like my parents taught me. Every emotion has a reason and a source. Still, I miss those frightening times, those ugly moods, that mix of irrational up and devastating low. I miss them because they were mine.

ELISSA

237   um—okay last question—so.

238   do you think your attitude toward sex will be different after college and.

239   is there anything. that you might. do differently

INTERVIEWEE

240   well I think.

241   giving head? <laughs>

242   I find giving head

243   after college is weird—

244   like—

245   when you're in the business world—

246 I dunno it just seems weird to me

247 it seems like more of a college thing—

248 um—so I don't pla—

249 well I di—

250 I don't plan on doing that now—

251 'cause I don't like it but—

252 it just seems more degrading

253 when you're out of college 'cause.

254   when you're in college.

255 you experiment and things like that—

256 and find. what you like.

257 I don't think.

258 a lot of girls like giving head. so—

<Omitted: she needs to be reminded of the question. Resumes at 26:06.>

INTERVIEWEE

259 and I think—

260 well after college you'll be older—

261 um. I'll be looking more

262 for a relationship—

263 and not that fuck buddy.

264 that I do. look for right now—

265 um—hopefully—

266 and like I think it's.

267 more acceptable in college

268 to be promiscuous—

269 than. outside of college. so—

270 I'll prob'ly try to tone that down.

271 um. just for the sake of looks.

272 and—y'know—

273 people not calling me a slut.

274 y'know. because—

275 you can be a slut in college and then—

276 y'know—

277 people will be like.

278 oh that's funny—

279 but if you're a slut outside of college—

280 it's like oh—

281 who d'you think you are—

282 you're a big slut <laughter>

283 so yeah—

284 the end <laughs>

ELISSA

285 the end

286 anything more to say?

INTERVIEWEE

287 um—

288 yeah guys need to learn.

289 how to please their women [yeah]

290 'cause that's that's a big problem—

291 and Chuck needs to go fuck himself

ELISSA

292 dude dude—

293 if we're talking about guys

294 who need to go FUCK themselves.

295 well I can't think of anybody right now

INTERVIEWEE

296 actually all guys

297 need to go fuck themselves

ELISSA

298 the end

INTERVIEWEE

299 the end.

300 motherfuckers

‹END OF RECORDING›

It's been years—three, five, one thousand—since I could say I am without regret. Even after I can shed a peel of old skin and feel as raw as the shiny pink under the dead, sunburned top layer, I am not really new. Not at first. It will happen after I start to forget how the old feelings were, and have less emotion in me.

Mary of Egypt, fucker of pilgrims, resident of the desert, patroness of penitents, hear me: maybe, in God's eyes—if God exists, if you do—maybe a hard-ass God would feel that I let the rape happen. I did not want him to break my face, or anything else visible. And let's say I could have stopped myself all the other times. I'm no virgin martyr. I've lived to know orgasms, homemade guacamole, Deschutes Brewery's limited-edition 11% alcohol by volume Abyss Imperial Stout, Seroquel and Lexapro, Dr. Dre's *The Chronic*, falling asleep on a pillow-top mattress, the best macaroni and cheese recipe on earth, Air Force Ones and Dunks, the self-righteous satisfaction of farmers' market shopping, Netflix. A hundred thousand pleasures. No god would want me to choose death.

Mary didn't have to. Mary didn't just lose her virginity—she notched her bedpost down to a toothpick. Then she removed herself from the world and made it right. I want to do that: do my penance and forgive myself, and let the world, or any god who's watching, follow my lead.

I might have dreamed it or I might have just thought it up, but I know it never happened, Kurt and I going into the woods. At a canal campsite we were both bipolar. I was on a rock jutting out of the water with my hands on my hips; he was on land, taking my picture. Of him there were already enough photos to make a nearly complete record. Then we built a fire. His forehead, sweaty strands of hair glued across, was too close to the flames but he was too superhuman to feel the heat. He provoked the flames with a stick.

We were toxic and docile. We were radioactive and stable. I wanted to tell him, let's stop taking our pills. I'll wear high heels and you'll stalk with a machete. In the water our pills will dissolve like fish food. But I know our backs are buckled to the bottles in the bathroom, our brains are pickled in squeezed-out chemicals, our ribs would crack against the heaving of our hearts if we let them.

When the dream was over he was dead and I was still alive.

Criteria for a comeback:
1. No longer intoxicated in public.
2. Lost weight/looks hot.
3. Doing shit worthy of the pages of *People* (*Star* does not count).

4. Appears on talk shows publicly asserting that the past has been left behind.

5. Behaves/has learned how to get out of cars without flashing vadge.

6. Critics are using words like "triumphant" and "redemption."

7. No more drama.

I used to pray to Kurt sometimes. I believed in ghosts, the violent ones in my books of scary stories, so I thought he could kill me in my sleep. Since then I have grown into my brain and learned that Britney and I have brains as similar as left and right palms. Eventually, when Britney's documentary *For the Record* came out, I heard her say, "I cannot see how I got through that," and maybe that is part of the mystery of mental illness: bipolar disorder is incurable, and for some of us, for Kurt, it's so active and malignant that it becomes terminal, a disease that will end the life of the sufferer. Britney and I will just have to hope that it won't come to suicide for us, and accept that we'll be gulping down pills until we die.

A Cascade Autobiography

PART 14

My Navajo friend Chester said Navajos keep getting gall-bladder disease because of all the sheep they eat. Navajo is not Cowlitz, not at all, so I don't know anything about that, but I know I used to show my four little white incisions to anyone who would look. I had surgery in college and it messed up my digestion, making me unable to eat without feeling as though I've been kicked in the stomach. The logical solution was to stop eating. I began to wish the biological urge to eat didn't run me.

When I came out of gallbladder surgery, I could only think about pain and apology. "I'm sorry for not making any sense," I told the nurses, "and I'm at seven." Morphine couldn't bring my pain number down. It didn't matter that I wasn't going to die, or that nothing was going to change but my digestion, because until the Demerol shot into my veins, my pure pain was of the same substance as the pain Tumalth or Mary felt when the Cascades were murdered and scattered. But my pain, born on an operating table and relieved with rest and an intravenous drip, lacked purity and substance. I chose this pain; I knew the possible outcomes of signing my name, and except for a little digestive disturbance, I'm fine.

The summer I was at American University, I made a show of not being able to eat meat or cheese or any animal fats because of my gallbladder, and the other Indians would nod and say, "Oh yeah, my aunt's got her gallbladder out." I didn't often mention that my white dad had his gallbladder out too, or that I took birth control pills from age fifteen on and played God with my hormones, and used antibiotics that cause "internal malignancy" to combat acne for years,

153

all of which point to the development of gallbladder disease. If my fate is predetermined, I can do nothing wrong.

In school, when the white kids would get mad at me for being Native and not looking it, which seemed to mean misusing it to get an advantage I didn't need, I wanted to ask them what to do. I think they wanted me to forget I was Indian. Would that entail getting to pick another way to allocate the three-thirty-seconds of my blood that will be freed up when I'm not Indian anymore? Am I supposed to stop calling my mom? Or should I issue a poll: How can I be white enough for you, and what do I do now with all the self-tanning foam that never gets me brown enough?

"Washuta" is one vowel away from "Washita." Google that. It's a river in Oklahoma. You'll also find that it was the location of an 1868 battle in which Colonel George Armstrong Custer attacked a Cheyenne Village. Even though Chief Black Kettle raised the white flag, he and his wife and a hundred other Indians were shot dead.

Every summer, Chief Tumalth's descendants get together at Beacon Rock in Southern Washington's Columbia Gorge. Beacon Rock remains where the Columbia River stripped away the fat from an ancient volcano, leaving the world's second largest free-standing rock behind. Lewis and Clark reached it and named it in 1805. Everything in Washington is volcanic and everything is renamed and re-owned. I don't know what Beacon Rock was called, but Wy'East became Mount Hood, Pahto is now Mount Adams, La-wa-la-clough is Mount Saint Helens.

We gather in an outdoor pavilion and eat all different kinds of potato salad. Still, years after moving to Washington, I meet unfamiliar relatives there. At first, few truly felt like family. I would wander among people I felt I was supposed to know but couldn't because they lived on the opposite coast. I understood that they didn't have to love me, which is hard on a girl from New Jersey. But after attending every year, I learned names and relations, and a family feeling began to percolate. I got the hang of it and started to see that there's something special about being invited to belong.

We cluster under Tumalth's name and stare at the family tree posted on the side of the pavilion, but everything I've learned about him came from books. I only heard from my mother's mouth that he was a chief, a term nearly as blurry as "Indian princess." I grew up thinking that chiefs should have their faces on textbook pages and T-shirts, like Sitting Bull. I couldn't find Tumalth in my book of *Great Speeches by Native Americans,* or in any of the books at the county library. I began to worry that my family had made up the whole thing.

When my doctor finally put his finger on the bipolar diagnosis, pulled there like a knowing planchette skidding across an Ouija board to a spectral message, I felt relieved to have finally arrived at an answer. It was as though it had been working its way out of my spinal cord. I quit my part-time tribal relations job at USDA soon after I was diagnosed, partly because I thought I had a lot of shit to work out, partly because I just wanted to finish school, and partly because I didn't need to work so hard at being Native now that I had something else to work on. During my last week there, I found out that in my office of eleven people, I was one of three bipolars. Nobody questioned me or asked to see proof. They told me that if I wanted to talk, their cubicles were always open.

At that time, I became increasingly frustrated with the notion of Indianness, feeling so far away from the reservations I clumsily fictionalized. I abandoned story drafts soon after completing them. I thought that if I read more about the history of Native Americans—Hopi, Mohawk, Chippewa, no matter—I would almost get my blood boiling enough to reduce it down to a steaming, potent syrup that would contain some legitimate Indian essence. But blood's not really made of history. Once I started seeing the college clinic psychiatrist, he pulled out my blood and showed me what was really in it, glanced at each trace mineral in the lab results, each lurking marker, but his eyes were focused on the good stuff, the chemicals he'd put there. I don't know if I believe in "Indian blood," but at times, I have wished I could test positive for it when the phlebotomist pulled my blood every month, checking to make sure my lithium levels aren't high enough to pickle my kidneys. Instead, the doctor only ever reads off results that sound like the bottom of a deep quarry, as though my body collects stones.

When I was thirteen, I told Grandma Kate that we were going down to the river to see Tsagaglalal, known in English as She Who Watches, a stone petroglyph of a woman's face. Grandma corrected my pronunciation. In her mouth the word was made of sounds I would never hear again. My mother always said Grandma didn't speak the language. If she did, it was a secret she needed to keep. She raised her children white. I'm told that this was a good idea in the fifties and sixties in Washington. I wish she had taught me what she knew, but the urge to take the sum of what you are and keep it like a secret is not foreign to me.

My mother and her twin sister were beautiful all-American girls. In high school, well-liked and active, they attained the valedictorian and salutatorian spots in their class. They've never stopped being beautiful. In their yearbook photos for Girl of the Month and Girl of the Year their smiles say, "We can do *anything.*"

My breakdown:

3/16 Irish

5/32 Scottish

1/8 Polish

1/8 Ukrainian

1/8 German

1/8 Dutch

1/16 Cascade

1/32 Cowlitz

1/32 Welsh

1/32 French

Little known fact: my last name is Ukrainian.

At the Native research symposium I attended in grad school, the presenter who spoke about the connection between rape and genocide talked about sexual violence in the US-Mexico borderlands. Rapes of Native women go unreported. Is this so unusual? I suspect that there is no place in the world where even a small fraction of the rapes that occur are brought to justice. This problem has something to do with the genocide of the Native people and something to do with having a vagina, being the fucked rather than the fucker. Knowing that I wasn't alone made me feel worse, because it meant I was just another trampled member of an angry chorus.

There is a strange prestige associated with calling oneself a rape victim. For some judgmental onlookers to be comfortable with the application of words like "rape" and "sexual assault" to another person's experience, the incident must meet certain criteria (none of which are universally agreed upon): maybe force, usually a clear, vocal "no." For me to use the label took great effort. First, I had to ask professionals—therapists, counselors, a phone voice from a rape counseling service—whether I could use the term. They said I could, but still, I was afraid. The bipolar label, too, is special. Getting a diagnosis was easier than getting a rapist's indictment would have been. The only life the diagnosis could ruin was mine.

The strongest indicator of bipolar disorder is family history. But nobody in my family has been diagnosed. There was never even suspicion. My psychiatrist said it had to come from somewhere and asked me to think hard. "No," I told him, "it had to have started with me." I didn't want to reach back and find that I had to share this with some stranger. I wanted my brain to be only mine.

I Will Perfect Every Line
Until My Profile Is Flawless

HTTP://WWW.MATCH.COM/PROFILE/EDIT

LAST MODIFIED: 4/9/2009

WAXLEAVES [54]

I LOVE SNEAKERS AND SKYLINES. [55]

FOR FUN: [56]

I write nonfiction. I collect and wear beautiful, colorful sneakers. I love clothing and creating incredible outfits. I used to have radio shows at college, 80s new wave and mid- to late-90s hip-hop, and I still love music. I sing karaoke. [57]

MY JOB:

I study fiction and nonfiction in a graduate (Master's) program. That's my primary thing. I also work as a barista at a bakery-cafe. [58]

---

54   A screen name I've been using since high school, based on a line of a shitty poem I wrote.

55   If you don't have a catchy tagline, you have nothing. People pay other people money to work on this shit.

56   The idea of fun to most Match.com males is vomit-inducing and impossible for me to even pretend to have an affinity for. Most of them like to hike, surf, and take advantage of opportunities to wear heavy-duty man-sandals. I do not hike, surf, or do anything that could merit me the label of "active," except for actively disliking outdoorsy shit. I also don't go to the movies, bowl, watch stand-up, go to amusement parks, or engage in activities involving dogs, so my strategy in this section is to appear as "quirky" as possible so that I can get out of having to go on hikes.

57   True answer: I drink, I eat, I play Nintendo, I write. Twice a week, I sing karaoke at a gay bar that no guy I'm dating will ever want to come to with me. I write essays that no guy will want to read, and I read them to audiences while I still can, before I have to start pretending I never fucked and only came into existence five minutes before meeting my future partner. I also enjoy filling my weekly pill-box with my prescription antipsychotics, antidepressants and lithium, all of which I currently practice explaining to others in preparation for justifying to a future partner when he asks me, "But haven't you ever thought about going off all that nasty shit? It's so bad for you."

58   Disclosing both grad school and the food service job is key. If I'm mentioning just the job, I sound like a loser, but if I'm mentioning grad school, it's important to at least provide the appearance of working my way through it, even if the café job only keeps me in beer money. I don't want to sound spoiled, so I don't want to mention that I'm getting through grad school using my parents' cash that they didn't spend on my undergrad years because I got a full ride. Dates don't respect that—they resent it.

MY RELIGION:

I was Catholic. Now I'm not. I might become religious again someday, I'm open to it.[59]

FAVORITE HOT SPOTS:

Capitol Hill bars.[60] Downtown restaurants.[61] Crazy bars[62] or little coffee shops,[63] it's all good.[64] I'm comfortable in dives or upscale restaurants, don't really have a preference.

FAVORITE THINGS:

My Reebok Grace mid-tops. Fencing. Avocado, tomato, hummus, and provolone on ciabatta. Coffee, Pabst. *Law & Order: SVU* in huge doses. My coats. My balcony. The Mountain Goats. Driving. Above all, writing.[65]

LAST READ:

American Psycho. Terrifying.[66]

ABOUT MY LIFE AND WHAT I'M LOOKING FOR:[67]

I'm chatty, different, smart, and interesting.[68] I'm devoted and passionate—I ended up in one of the top grad writing programs in the country.[69] My apartment is very

---

59   Complete bullshit. I know I'll never be religious again. This is what I'm saying about flexibility, but it's also true that I've never been certain that God does not exist, and for this reason, "I'm open to it" is more honest than "I've never been outdoorsy, but I want to be": I can't rule out the possibility of ending up as an old Catholic lady after my vulva has enjoyed as many vibrator-induced orgasms as possible.

60   So they know I like to drink. Guys only want to date chicks who drink.

61   So they know I'm worth it.

62   Really, though, I drink.

63   But I'm not totally crazy; I'm sometimes also low-maintenance.

64   And easygoing! You'd barely even know I'm fucking batshit crazy.

65   The only completely true paragraph in this motherfucker.

66   After I recently read *American Psycho*, dating started to terrify me more than ever before. Even though my dating life has been riddled with terror for years, some of which brought me to Match, and none of which changed my habits or made me aware of the importance of personal safety, there was something about reading about trusting girls sawed into pieces that really freaked me out.

67   The true answer: after twenty months in Seattle, all of them on the same meds, I've realized I have achieved some sort of stability. I'm not ready to take on the world, exactly, but I'm at least ready to kick it with a cool boy. The rapid cycling of my moods put incredible distance between my current self and the old ones—the girl bleeding on the bathroom floor in 2005, and the one bending swords into ribcages while her own heart heaved in 2006, and the jangling skeleton of 2007, and 2008's girl trapped in a box of shadows and scripted traumas. I became sick of it, just wanting to meet somebody.

68   When I first posted this profile, some guy called me out on this: "A little arrogant, are we?" to which I replied, "I don't do mock-humble." Apparently, though, I *did* do mock-confident.

69   Really, though, this is self-confident posturing, the result of too many sources urging me to work on feeling good about myself before asking any man to feel good about me. Men, I am told, do not

messy. I read *Cosmopolitan*; I also read literary theory.[70] I used to work for the federal government, in tribal relations. On a normal day, I wake up, work on my book/home-work, go to class, have some kind of fun outing.[71] I'm finishing grad school, so that will change things in a wonderful way.[72]

I write essays; I'm writing a memoir in essays. My stuff is kind of bold. Maybe you can read it when I get to know you better.[73]

I kind of like sitting in the dark when I'm at home. I'm not outdoorsy, but I'd like to be,[74] now that I'm in a city whose amazing natural surroundings helped to draw me to it.[75] So, let's go camping.[76] I don't like snow, but I'll put up with rain. During the summer, I sleep outside for a little while every day, when I can.[77] I grew up in a place where I could chill with nature as a kid—hang out with mushrooms and cedar trees, pick wineberries from the backyard, make forts in the thickets. I was also an indoor kid, reading about mermaids and stuff. I'm still all of that.

I'm an extremely independent person, most accustomed to being on my own, and I'd like to always remain independent, but I'd like to have a guy in my life, too.[78] I moved across the country in my car, picked Seattle as my new city despite all my connections

---

want to be with girls who don't feel good about themselves. I have made sure to let them know that I do, even if I don't.

70 I've never read lit theory in my life, but it sounds smart.

71 *I'm just so fucking fun.*

72 *My life is just so wonderful that a guy would be nuts if he didn't want to be in it.*

73 The inclusion of this line is a result of too many guys asking me, "What kind of stuff do you write? Can I read it?" The real answer is too inappropriate to say: "I'm working on an essay that's a reverse-chronological listing of the dudes I've fucked. It's a work in progress and something tells me you're not going to be a part of it."

74 Bullshit. I do not have any intention to ever go on a hike. I just figure I should say this, because almost every male profile mentions the outdoors. I wonder whether we're all buying into the lie.

75 True, but really, I'm content just to look at that shit from afar.

76 In my head, this sounds like me conceding an argument. *Fine*, honey—I haven't even met you, but I'm so lonely that I'll brave the woods if you want me to.

77 That has never happened. I might have dozed off while tanning by the pool, but reclining on a vinyl chair above concrete hardly counts as putting in some time in the great outdoors.

78 This, too, is what I figure guys wanted to hear, because the sentiment is completely in line with the male notion that had been bounced off me so often: "I want you when I want you, but not when you're feeling needy or premenstrual"; the ideal female response to this consists of, "I am a sex fiend unless I know I'm feeling cunty, or when you're out with the boys or otherwise having your 'man time,'" the idea being that a bitch should always be available to a man unless she's bleeding, vaginally or emotionally, but if he doesn't want her, she needs to respect his fucking space.

coated. So healthy and vital in appearance that you'd never know I had been starving myself for long enough that my menstruation had stopped. A desirable girl, someone you'd take to coffee in a second.][86]

CAPTION: GRAPHIC TEES, ANYONE? I'VE GOT MORE THAN A DOZEN AWESOME DESIGNS.

[Candid at 115 pounds. I am leaning against a friend's shoulder while laughing. Smile is broad, spontaneous, and devoid of the "say-cheese" awkwardness typical of posed photos in which the subject is forced to smile. Jacket from H&M's Madonna collection, white with a gold zipper. Cropped-out person is obviously male, and could appear to be a significant other.][87]

CAPTION: FUN TIMES WITH GOOD PALS

[Posed glamour shot in front of some statue in DC against blue sky, American flag waving in background. Long white coat, long hair, pink-framed sunglasses. This photo is my grandma's favorite of me. It was taken by a guy who urged me to pose naked for SuicideGirls photos.][88]

CAPTION: DURING MY TIME WORKING IN DC, GETTING MY JACKIE O. ON

[A close-up of my face. This, too, is from the skinny period. The look in my eyes is so earnest you'd have no trouble believing you were seeing the real me.]

CAPTION: CLOSE-UP! YOU CAN ALMOST SEE MY CONTACT LENSES. TAKEN AT WMUC, WHERE I DJED IN COLLEGE.

[A current photo; the only one taken within the past year. I stand in a doorway, hands gripping the frame, showing blood-red nails. Hot pink T-shirt on which THIS IS

---

86 "**Rule #6: Don't post an out-of-date photo.** Seriously, your date will notice the extra 20 pounds or 10-year age difference when you walk in the door. Be honest with who you are and what you currently look like. If you start off with misrepresentations, you're wasting your time! 'If you take your interaction to the next step with an actual live date, the person on the other end will likely feel deceived and angry,' says Botwinick. 'It's a setup for disaster, so be comfortable in your own skin and represent the real you for an honest start.' Before you post a photo, ask yourself: *If I were to meet someone for coffee today, could I look like that?* It will help you choose which photos best represent you online" (from "The Top 10 Online-photo Tips," *Happen*, Match.com's online magazine).

87 I just love to laugh.

88 "Cornell University researchers Jeffrey Hancock and Catalina Toma have scientifically confirmed what many of us would only sheepishly admit to others, if at all: our dating profile pictures aren't always accurate. To put it another way, they're sometimes a little *too* flattering. Hancock and Toma met with 54 straight singles in the flesh to verify that the photos they'd posted in their online profiles were accurate representations of each person's physical attributes. In doing so, they discovered that about one-third of the photos were judged to be inaccurate representations and most of those photos belonged to women" (from "How to Post Better Photos," *Happen*, Match.com's online magazine).

killed off most of the area's Native population in a single
summer. In 1855, at age twenty-five or so, Tumalth signed a
treaty in which he and many other signers gave up much of
their land. They would move to the Grand Ronde reserva-
tion, and although the US pledged to provide food and sup-
plies and even education, Tumalth didn't live long enough
to see the rapid trampling of these promises. A year later,
the Yakamas attacked the white settlement at the Cascades
of the Columbia, a single action in an ongoing war, and the
Cascades became entangled in the fight, despite the treaty,
because they lived there, and they were pissed off, and whites
had been settling where they didn't belong. Mary and her
sisters, daughters of Tumalth, would insist that their father
was wrongly accused, but still, he was hanged. His family
was enslaved by the Klamath Indians, later freed during a
US Army attack, and taken to Fort Vancouver. The soldiers,
in a baffling gesture, took up a collection of gold for the girls,
feeling bad about what happened to their dad.

I try to picture Tumalth, but I will never find his gleaming eyes in a sepia portrait or his last words transcribed in
a mass-market paperback. I can make guesses about the
aches of his guts as he stepped onto the scaffold, ready to
leave a world quickly emptying itself of familiar men. His
daughters and granddaughters would grow into a world
full of settler men who would roll into the women's lives
for a fertilization or a marriage, for long strings of nights
dappled with whiskey and cards, for the wife's trust land
to be tossed into his debts as though it were a bag of beads,
for the wife's shotgun stationed at the door to bar her hard-
partying husband from entering, for her threats of suicide
by knife and his wrangling for the blade. The women and
the men stared each other down across a deep gorge, novices
at everyday armistice. Five generations after Tumalth was
hanged for being Indian, being in charge, and being around,

I took for granted my undergrad university's "commitment to cultural diversity" and wailed about my schoolmates' bigotry. Tumalth had to leave his girls in a land of true discord. I cannot know even a sliver of it. The story is in the details, the traumas, the histories, not the titles and labels we apply and try to pass down without context. I've been searching for the story, the whole beast, the blessing, the burden.

Please Him, Part 2

The road to heaven is paved with meat:
the road to meat is not paved at all.
JOE WENDEROTH

LIVES OF THE SAINTS

When I was nineteen and twenty and still a virgin, I had a *Cosmo* subscription delivered to my first apartment. No longer did I have to sneak issues in secret, as I did when
I was too young to be worrying about keeping my hoo-ha toned. As an independent
young college woman, I knew I was too tight to have sex but I wanted to go into it prepared with sex tips. I wanted to know what five things to never tell my guy, twenty-one
naughty ways to give him the sex he's always dreamed of, the best five things to do with
his balls. Men and I had to be in opposition for sex to work, for humanity to operate.
When I finally lost my virginity, I learned that I was right. He beat my va-jay-jay like
an opponent in the ring. I lost.

When I was twenty-one, I went to the National Shrine in DC on my way home
from work. I crossed the Catholic University campus and saw people my age. We'd
been the same when we were kids, probably, but something had happened—I had
gone rotten. The basilica is tremendous, with its bulbous head, gold and statues. I
arrived too early for evening mass, so I went to the gift shop and bought some medallions. I hadn't been taught the catechism in years but I knew who my patron saints
would be, now that my life changed. I bought a steel chain and four medallions: Maria
Goretti, Agnes, Dymphna, and Cecilia. The priest's homily was about angels. I didn't
need to really listen to the rest; words triggered my legs to stand, sit, kneel. I arranged
my medallions in my palm and watched them. The women were frozen, standing,
robed, with arms spread or hands folded. Canonization had cemented them. Confessions were heard after mass, and even though I knew I could confess it all, cleanse my
soul, go back to the Church like nothing had ever happened, I wouldn't.

The story of Maria Goretti, the girl who was not-quite-raped and then murdered
and sainted, still doesn't make sense to me. She was a child and he was an adult. He
could have raped her if he had wanted to. The fight in her got her killed. Is that what
God wanted? Is that what he wanted for me? I knew that I had sinned by letting my
rape happen. But that didn't mean I was wrong to fear Damian's violence. If I brought

myself to confess that I had not done all I could, I would be doing my own violence. I did the right thing.

> When Jezebel learned that Jehu had arrived in Jezreel, she shadowed her eyes, adorned her hair, and looked down from her window. As Jehu came through the gate, she cried out, "Is all well, Zimri, murderer of your master?" Jehu looked up to the window and shouted, "Who is on my side? Anyone?" At this, two or three eunuchs looked down toward him. "Throw her down," he ordered. They threw her down, and some of her blood spurted against the wall and against the horses. Jehu rode in over her body and, after eating and drinking, he said: "Attend to that accursed woman and bury her; after all, she was a king's daughter." But when they went to bury her, they found nothing of her but the skull, the feet, and the hands. They returned to Jehu, and when they told him, he said, "This is the sentence which the Lord pronounced through his servant Elijah the Tishbite: 'In the confines of Jezreel dogs shall eat the flesh of Jezebel. The corpse of Jezebel shall be like dung in the field of the confines of Jezreel, so that no one can say: This was Jezebel.'"
> (2 Kings 9:30–37)

ELISSA WASHUTA, former virgin and sometimes martyr (1984–)
Patroness of victims of rape, the mentally ill. Elissa was born in New Jersey on the Feast of St. Catherine of Alexandria, virgin martyr who was tethered to a spiked wheel and then beheaded after refusing a royal marriage in exchange for denying the faith. Elissa never refused anything. On a cold night in 2005, Elissa was sleeping in her bed when a young man overcame her. She did not say she would rather die than submit. She will never offer him Christian forgiveness, does not love her enemy. She is called a martyr not because she was punished with death for maintaining her belief, but because she subjects herself to suffering and portrays herself as victim. We can learn from her life: die rather than submit, not to maintain your virginity, but to avoid being obsessed for life. Or, we can learn another meaning of martyrdom: sacrifice your pride, self-respect, and well-being in order to keep your life, the most important thing God ever gave you, a thing so important that your instincts override all. Elissa will never be a saint because her body overrode her devotion to God. She should have let the hopeful, innocent little Catholic schoolgirl inside of her die in that bed.

THE DIVINE MYSTERY

Catholicism is shot through with mystery, but unlike a detective novel, *The Catechism of the Catholic Church* offers no resolutions of the Church's mysteries by page 845. So much is unknowable; we must summon up so much faith if we want to buy into this. The Divine Mystery is only knowable through Divine Revelation, and that's just not going to happen for any of us earthly beings, this knowledge being beyond human understanding.

My existence is riddled with earthly mysteries. I want to know how a little rubbing on a tiny nugget of nerves between my legs can launch me into the stratosphere, make me speak in tongues, and why bad shit happens to good people, and how my brain works, and what every man I've ever been with has been thinking at any moment.

The real mystery, though, is my own brain, my own desire: I don't know why the hell I want to please the men who hurt me, who debase me, who hold me down and come on me even though it reminds me too much of porn for me to really want it, or stick their dicks so far down my throat I throw up a little but they don't notice and tell me to shut up when I say I want to stop so I keep going. My therapist calls this the "whatever effect": by saying to myself, "Whatever, I'll do this for him, it's not so bad," I default to his pleasure over mine. By design, I aim to please, like a slutty concierge.

> Upon my bed at night I sought him who my soul loves;
> I sought him, but found him not;
> I called him, but he gave no answer.
> "I will rise now and go about the city,
> in the streets and in the squares;
> I will seek him whom my soul loves."
> I sought him, but found him not.
> (Song of Solomon 3:1–2)

Holy Scripture affirms that man and woman were created for one another: *It is not good that the man should be alone.* The woman, "flesh of his flesh," i.e., his counterpart, his equal, his nearest in all things, is given to him by God as a "helpmate"; she thus represents God from whom comes our help. *Therefore a man leaves his father and his mother and cleaves to his wife, and they become one flesh.*

Conjugal love involves a totality, in which all the elements of the person enter—appeal of the body and instinct, power of felling and affectivity, aspiration of the spirit and of will. It aims at a deeply personal unity, a unity that, beyond union in one flesh, leads to forming one heart and soul; it demands *indissolubility* and *faithfulness* in definitive mutual giving.

That, right there, is exactly what I've always wanted. If you're so melted into him that you've become a single unit, what's wrong with trying to please your man, really?

The nuns told me many times that God built free will into the humans. We could walk out anytime. Of course, sitting in our desks in All Saints Regional, in plaid jumpers or gray slacks, we were not free to go. The ability to choose would come later. The Catechism is clear and explicit: *Man is rational and therefore like God; he is created with free will and is master over his acts.* But, of course, God doesn't like rejection. The opposites of love and obedience are evil and sin. No in-between exists. If there is no gray area between piousness and hellishness, I want to fail forever, make the best mistakes, feel all the pain and regret, because I have the freedom to act as a disobedient child, and I can't resist doing just that.

Freedom supposedly comes from doing good and choosing God, and choosing sin is slavery. One right choice, a million wrong ones—what kind of freedom is that? The Catholics say our freedom was part of God's great plan. As in the stable romantic relationships I've been in, his followers know that they can leave any time, but they're happier staying.

It's easy to be twenty-four and hate the Catholic Church. So I don't. I just don't show up.

But I can't stop being fascinated. I can't completely walk away. My history with the Church runs too deep. When I was a little kid, I believed. I had no doubt that the bland wafers turned into Jesus' body, or that the saints were carrying my prayers up through the atmosphere to his front door. When I reached the age of twelve, I lost the ecstatic love that I'd need to continue to devote my life to God, and so I broke up with him. Sometimes, I wish I still believed. I love all those holy cards and saint statues and the structure of the mass. I used to love hearing so much Polish at church, and knowing that for my fellow parishioners, being Catholic had little to do with showing off one's love of Jesus to the neighbors and everything to do with being Polish. Sometimes I wish I could go back to being Catholic, because I'd have something to believe in outside my fucked-up life, and I could know that everything happens according to some great plan for me. But I can't pick and choose which laws of the Church I'm going to follow, I can't stop masturbating, and I can't make myself believe.

Kateri Tekakwitha—*She Who Bumps into Things,* the half-blind girl—did not fit her moniker of *the Lily of the Mohawks* until her spirit was gone from her body and the husk turned white. She carried out a scarred-over life, seeking only to cover the old smallpox spatter with fresh wounds, self-induced, acute but impermanent. Some now say she did not give up her traditional beliefs, but added to her faith, escaping to Catholicism after turning down an arranged marriage with a Mohawk man. To Kateri, the Church served the purpose that John Smith served to Disney's Pocahontas as she defied her father's demand to marry the "so serious" Kocoum, and Kateri, like Pocahontas, fell hard for the magnetic visitors and their enchanting yarns. She grasped burning coals between her toes, daring herself to relax, and prayed for hours outdoors on her knees in the northern snow. In 1680, her choice to sleep for three successive nights on a bed of thorns while sick with a fever may have quickened her death.

Everyone around Kateri told her to stop hurting herself, but she wouldn't, could only press on, push harder, burn hotter, and strive to become so close to the Lord that there would barely be a membrane between her humble soul and *Karonhià:ke,* the vast Sky World of the Lord. Beyond every saint's stock desire for mortification that they call sacrifice, saying the pain is offered up to God like a birthday gift, in Kateri's story, I see a desire to exert control over a changing world filled with French and Dutch colonizers upending the indigenous natural order. While Kateri watched her family die, the Jesuit clerics offered a way out of the suffering, having some sort of powers—immunity to the foreign diseases—that allowed them to survive while the Natives fell to disease.

Something harder to explain takes place between the whip and the rib, between the knife tip and thin skin, that has nothing to do with pleasing God by gifting him abstract pain. What lover wants such a morbid present as a pool of blood or a patch of frostbitten skin?

I have not wrapped my body in the hair shirt, have never bound my bones with the iron girdle, but I may as well have. I strapped myself to my grief for a long time and beat it into the folds of my skin. Every sexual misstep was a line of a litany petitioning some savior for intercession—*Mercy of God, inexhaustible source of miracles, have mercy on us.*

I thought I could flog the pain out of myself, and at the same time, I thought it would take a miracle to fix me.

Lord, I am not worthy to receive you, but only say the word and I shall be healed.

Once I fall in love, or even approach it, my hands change. They aim to please, driven by my heart, rove across the man's body and press a message into his skin: *I just want to make you happy.* There is no *give head to get head,* no *What have you done to deserve a hand job tonight?* running unspoken through my brain.

The authors of the Catechism were right when they wrote, "Love is the fundamental and innate vocation of every human being." But they would probably advise readers to love God above all. I must worship myself first. Loving God takes faith; loving myself takes a different kind. I know, at least, that I am real, but to really love myself means knowing I am worth it even when I fall. I am a believer.

After my last breakup, a painful end to a short relationship that had me optimistic,[104] I considered whether I was a glutton for too much hope and punishment. I liked to carry out the little gestures that I thought would be meaningful for some eventual Mister Right, like bringing him a pot of flowering lavender tea with the New Jersey mug I noticed made Sam smile. I knew he was going to end things soon, peering into his ironed-on smiles, but I kept holding on, maybe just to get some practice in for when the right guy would come along. I finally began to understand what the nuns meant to tell me: do it because you want to, so badly, because you can't not, because the sounds he makes when your touch is working on him are just as pleasurable to you as his touch working on you. With Sam, I did not feel this pleasure, but I practiced for when I would get it. There seemed to be nothing wrong with trying to please that perfect man *Cosmo* knew I could catch and keep if you played it right.

I wasn't certain that I would be worthy to receive that perfect man when he would eventually arrive. I sometimes walked with a limp, I refused to give head, my gut swelled with lactose intolerance, my lips were always chapped. Sometimes I still wandered and sobbed and my brain did violence to itself. No matter. My smeared soul was visible from space. That perfect man might tell me that me up and down is the way of the brain. Stability is a wave, not a line.

---

104   See "Faster Than Your Heart Can Beat," #24.

Dating Sam, I felt more ready than I had ever been. When he and I broke up, it wasn't because I did the wrong thing with my tongue. He was checking out as I crawled toward him, ignoring *Cosmo*'s advice to never look desperate, talking endlessly to voicemail. When a man stops answering, you can never have faith that he loves you back, even if you think of his ways as mysterious and miraculous, explaining away the fact that you've lost him. Believing in God means that you can know for every second of the rest of your life that God loves you more than anyone on earth ever could. When I was a kid, I thought the weekend morning sunlight in my bedroom was God shining through my window. Now I go to sleep wondering whether anyone loves me who doesn't have to, until my cat lifts her paw to touch my face, as she does as I stop paying attention to her when I'm falling asleep. I say, "I love you, Dollie."

The real mystery is the cycle of romantic need, the feeling of not being enough. As Sam became less available, my panic became less about Sam and more about my desirability. I practiced hard, but the next man might not love me for it, either. In the weeks after the breakup, driving home from work every evening, I said, "I am enough. I am enough. I am enough." I prayed to myself, asking for the brain's intercession on behalf of the heart's troubles. I know that I am enough, but I spend lonely nights wandering around strange Seattle bars, staring at strangers' faces lit by dim bulbs, looking for some other level of access. It shakes my faith. I seek no savior now, not one in the sky who will wrap his hands around my soul, not one on this earth who will wrap his arm around my shoulders. Comfortably unattached, I walk and chant, touch my own hands, waiting for something to be revealed. In those moments, alone, walking, driving, I hear an answer, because I have in myself something more substantial than faith alone, something I never got from God when I prayed and never heard so much as an echo: I say, "I am enough," and in the weight of my hair pulling on my scalp, the brush of my thighs, the pain in my knees as I walk, I hear my response: *Yes. Maybe. Probably. Yes.*

I've followed the self-love lessons to the letter. I've loved myself hard and long. Nowadays, when someone else wants to reach me, they get a perpetual busy signal while I whisper sweet nothings to myself late into the night.

A Cascade Autobiography

PART 16

*Elissa Washuta's history of mood swings; erratic and irrespon-
sible behavior, including promiscuity; and episodes of depression and mania, sometimes simultaneously; determine the
diagnosis of bipolar disorder, mixed, despite the absence of
family history.*

My entire sexual history has taken place from age twenty
onward. Additions upon my foundation meant looking
back to the partners who came before. Recovery meant
no longer connecting every partner to my first, and bit by
bit, forgetting.

It took some time to get the hang of being simultaneously
white and Indian. But I had to be *something,* so I searched
for an identity to sink into. Before I knew I was bipolar, and
could settle into that, I had the rape. It was bloody and violent and it was an injustice of the kind my ancestors knew, I
used to think.

For a while, I had to make the rape fit into my life as
an Indian. It was nice to have a straightforward, academic
explanation to fall back on, one involving a history of violent oppression and subjugation, something about inherited
ancestral consciousness, something about how the guy who
raped me was English and could trace his ancestry back to
the first English settlers. Something I could tell myself so it
wasn't my own malfunction, neurosis, weakness, character
flaw, not my own fault.

I have tried to stuff all my reasoning into a small shell
and pull out nuggets of non-wisdom like, *That boy colo-
nized my brown body.* But the rape wasn't really anything

like what happened one hundred and fifty years ago at the Cascades of the Columbia River, because unlike Tumalth's broken-up generation, I got much better.

There is no test for bipolar disorder. I offer no proof, no card with my name and a rainbow brain scan image. If my disorder is akin to my Indianness at all, it's because I never asked for it, but because I see my brain and mind as most people don't, as two separate circles of hell, I wouldn't have it any other way. I am bipolar in a way that real Indians are really Indian: at thirteen, I knew I was bipolar without being told, before anyone else caught on. I have been too close to losing everything and then reprieved on the scaffold.

Six months into my drug treatment, I told my psychiatrist that people were telling me I might just be moody and I thought they were wrong. "They are wrong," he said. "You are sick, bipolar, and you need to be medicated. I am absolutely sure." And that sureness was just what I wanted.

The doctors keep asking about my family. They want to know who was bipolar before me. I imagine Tumalth, the twenty-five-year-old headman, in a psychiatrist's office, staring at his ankles, divulging his anxiety about the future. I hear Mary shaking a pill bottle like a rattle. I can't tell the doctors what they want to hear; we were without diagnoses until I fell. Bipolar disorder has the clinical film of a white man's invention, so I don't tell the doctors what I know about Abbie armed with shotgun, turning her knife against herself, or her husband—my great-grandfather—who perhaps slipped sips of liquor into my blood. I have found no exact place in the DSM-IV for the woman, expecting the birth of my grandma, who takes a pair of scissors to bed with her every night, wanting no white woman to mess with her. There is no act of neurochemical balancing that can restore order to their dismantled world. I do not think I was predestined for brokenness—this world of ours has shown itself to have no sense of order to make such a feat possible—but I'm learning to talk to the ancestors, listen for answers, stay awake in dreams, and let those loved ones erase the muddy corners of my brain so I might learn all over again how to know anything at all.

The Global Positioning Effect

Pharmaceutical wonders are at work
but I believe only in this moment
of well-being. Unholy ghost,
you are certain to come again.

JANE KENYON, "HAVING IT OUT WITH MELANCHOLY"

You do not have to be good.
You do not have to walk on your knees
for a hundred miles through the desert, repenting.
You only have to let the soft animal of your body
    love what it loves.
Tell me about despair, yours, and I will tell you mine.

MARY OLIVER, "WILD GEESE"

Tonight I go for a drive. The radio says that every day from here on out will be nice and springlike. In Seattle, the weather changes day-to-day like rapid cycling moods. Yesterday everyone was talking about what they heard today would be like—my classmates said eighties, the DJ said eighty-eight this morning, the grocery store cashier said eighty-seven. The year after my birth, 1985, set the record high at eighty-four. My skin could not put a number on the heat of the day, or the cool of tonight.

My city guidebook said never to call Seattle the Emerald City, despite its obvious greenness, so as not to sound like a tourist. Today's tea-like air asks for recognition of its contribution to the city's jewel-like glimmer. All day, in the humid air, the trees' leaves baked and the essential oils were diffused. At eleven at night, the smell remains when my cat wants me to sleep so she can curl up next to my knees. I want to go for a drive.

I head west first, to the residential neighborhoods I never visit because the freeway separates us. My areas of familiarity in the city amount to the size of fingernails on an open hand. I need to know more. For the first time, I want to feel that I live somewhere, not just through possession of a state driver's license, but through knowing the turns, expecting the buildings that will appear.

In DC, I avoided only the rough Southeast quadrant; inside the bowels of the L'Enfant Plaza Metro Station, deep underground, a Green Line sign pointing in the direction of Southeast/Anacostia is tagged with the scrawl "9ᵀᴴ WARD." But I have been everywhere else, on foot or in my car, and became most familiar with the government sector, where there is barely a place to get a sandwich, and where tourists seek out museum art and cherry blossoms; the downtown business district, as unremarkable as an unwrinkled navy blue suit; and the Northwest quadrant, whose embassies I drove past while manic to clear my head some nights. Citywide, the cherry trees often thwarted tourists' plans by blooming early and dropping their flowers in the rain.

I have at least one story for each DC neighborhood. Seattle has given me things to remember, in my two years here, but I won't know what memories are most essential without moving away. The city is like a cluster of cubbies in a kindergarten classroom, each with a different toy and lunchbox inside. Buses take riders from place to place, but not as swiftly as the DC Metro that snaked under my cubicle and made the neighborhoods seem so close they almost overlapped. Busing works for my commute, but when my brains are feeling this carbonated, I must drive. Driving is, for me, a solitary activity. Quarantined by chrome and glass, I can try to escape my moods without infecting anyone else. For the first time since moving to Seattle, I am experiencing a mixed episode—a bipolar relapse. Tonight, an old habit in a new city: driving around without a plan, feeling a need to take my skull off like a hat.

From downtown, I try to find an unfamiliar neighborhood. I have heard of this place called Magnolia, on the west edge of the city, where people have money and pretty houses. I have never gone there to drink or eat, have never driven through on the way to someone else, and I don't know how to get there. My city guide says, "Since the only ways in are by bridge or Dravus Street, most people write the whole place off as hard to reach, like an island."

Downtown, a minute after I start heading for the freeway to take me home, I see a sign for Magnolia. My brain sparkles more than the city lights when I take the exit. Even though I don't see a single magnolia tree—do they even grow out here?—I know when I've arrived. "The namesake tree of the neighborhood was a case of misidentification. From offshore, madrone trees with their peeling bark looked like magnolias to early explorers, and the name stuck." I get it: the explorers came here, figuring what they knew back East applied here, but then it wasn't true.

In the dark I can make out leaves gleaming like windshields, windshields gleaming like the surface of the Sound. I know the water is nearby—all around—and I have to find it. When I first brushed my hand across the cold surface of the Pacific, my dad told me I was special, because most people never touched two oceans. My whole child-hood was about water: the water I lived by, and the water that held the fish my dad cut open. I want to know where this strange Pacific water is, but for now, I stick to the speed limit and look at the houses.

My travel guide says, "Perfect topiaries have earned Magnolia the nickname 'Whoville,' after Dr. Seuss." I am glad that I don't see any. Perfection is hard to stomach.

Magnolia Boulevard seems like as good a place as any to drive. Somehow, though, I get lost, pulled toward the center of town, or what looks like the center of town, since I see a lit-up Tully's Coffee sign. It is the first business I've seen in Magnolia. I want to see whether they have a Starbucks, too. I am a barista in a city of baristas. I do not work at Starbucks or Tully's. People are supposedly serious about their coffee here, but the customers at Grateful Bread only order lattes. Tall nonfat latte, please; grande two-percent mocha; the foamy, aerated milk hides the espresso. Customers who order for-here lattes sit at wobbly little tables and don milk mustaches, as though they're preschoolers on a snack break.

I turn out of the small town center and head downhill. The Sound comes into view, a lit-up ferry in the center, like a plastic charm in the center of a cupcake. When I pull over and park, I become aware of the people in the houses along the street; the people all over Magnolia; all over the city. These are the people who talk about composting and tell me to exercise, a run around Greenlake would do me some good, and they want to know if the milk I'm steaming is organic, and they think yoga pants are real pants. Seattle is Amazon.com, Microsoft, Nintendo, Washington Mutual (or, it was, at one time), Nordstrom, Safeco, Costco. In Trenton, New Jersey, a red-lettered, glow-ing sign hangs on a bridge over the Delaware River and reads, "TRENTON MAKES, THE WORLD TAKES." Seattle might be the opposite: nothing, exactly, is made here, but things are consumed—only top-shelf things, free-range things, eco-friendly green things, fit-friendly and diet-friendly things. I don't know why Seattle people are so different from grumpy, tube-socks-and-pantyhose-wearing, non-organic-soft-pretzel-eating, never-recycling DC people. And I don't know why, despite my love of whole grains, I don't fit in here.

Since moving to Seattle, I have never been for a drive for the sake of driving and head-clearing. This was Maryland behavior, mixed-state behavior, lost-count-of-swal-lowed-anxiety-pills behavior. I used to drive from Maryland into the heart of DC, up and down the state-named streets. The Capitol Beltway was a ring more powerful than

Tolkien's. Everything that mattered was inside. The world was split into Beltway insiders and outsiders, power defined by location in relation to a road that goes nowhere.

During the drives, I felt even and unremarkable, no longer made of fluttering gills in need of oxygen. Driving with the windows down helped, but it was not until I reached DC's thoroughly-planted Northwest quadrant that my lungs got what they needed. In the near-darkness, the trees' leaves were almost black. The dewy, preened lawns exhaled when I passed. I went home when I felt that I had driven for long enough that the movement helped to distract my brain from its sickness and the crackling in my head had stopped.

I've been mostly stable for almost my entire time in Seattle. As a new resident, not yet stable, I wasn't comfortable enough here to go for a drive. I didn't have my PS yet, either, so even short trips grew long and frustrating. Then my new Seattle psychiatrist got my drugs right, and I was mostly better, and I only drove when I needed to get somewhere. Now I leak. My brain drips from my eyes. I thought it would come out more like a paste, or pus, not clear tears. Mucous brain slides out of my nostrils. I keep opening my eyes wider and wider, trying to wipe discreetly, so that I might not notice that I'm crying. I've cried every day for three fucking weeks.

"Landslides have afflicted the neighborhood more than once," the travel guide says, "pulling million-dollar homes down the hillside."

The house on my left is front-lit, the way the embassies are in DC, as if to show that these buildings are not just domiciles or workspaces: they are something to see. This house sits on uneven land. Magnolia is nothing like the wealthy suburbs I knew on the East Coast, because there, each house sits on a plot that could be any other plot. When my grandparents moved from Pennsylvania back to New Jersey, to a retirement community called Brookfield, they chose a piece of land, then a house model, then a color. Two similar models could not be next to each other on the street. But here, the houses are distinctly, but not glaringly, different. They are built to fit the land. Trees crouch around the homes at different angles, different heights, but never too high, never obscuring the view of the water.

Everyone's inside lights are off, and outside lights are on. I turn on my GPS and tell it to take me home. The lady inside silently considers my request. Against houses, like hands curled into funny shapes illuminated by flashlights against dark walls, trees make shadows. I must look suspicious, in my trucker hat and black hoodie, and I don't want anyone to call the cops, so I move on.

In the past two years, I have met other bipolars. Friends, friends of friends. A girl who lost it halfway through senior year of college, a guy with scars on his arms, my hospitalized ex-boyfriend, others who tell no stories. I wonder what makes the secret slip so much more often in Seattle than in Maryland. Maybe we're just getting older, and realizing that secrets are pointless. Now, I'm not alone, but I'm not special anymore, either.

I want to get back to Magnolia Boulevard, the wide street that lies like a limp arm along the shoulders of the Sound, but I end up at a gated estate. My GPS, still speechless, perches on the dash like a teacher at the front of a classroom who quietly waits for his students to figure out an answer and raise their hands with guesses. I turn around and find a new street. It keeps getting smaller, the land portions smaller, but even as I maneuver the car between cars parked on the streets in the absence of driveways, I know that the houses obscure a view of the water that is worth millions. I know, too, that my body is supposed to feel insignificant in comparison to this broad stretch of water and the mountains beyond. I am training myself to understand that in the grand scheme of things, I am not important, but I know that mountains do not have minds. I have no Native wisdom, no Western religion, so I am all I have.

But there are billions of us, each his own personal universe. I look out for number one. There is no one I would take a bullet for. I will grow up, and that will change.

I am lost. I have to piss. Bumps keep jarring the car, making the Pearl Jam CD skip. I have had this album since I was seventeen. Back then, I wanted to move to Seattle. The songs sounded like evergreens. Eddie Vedder sings that there's no crime in escape; I took my yearbook quote from this song. I am only seven years older than I was then, but I have become an old lady with old lady knees, a worn woman with a tired brain and a calcified heart. My GPS finally suggests, "Please drive to highlighted route," and throws a fat pink line up on the screen. An impenetrable line of homes and trees lies between the highlighted route and me.

Changing locale from Maryland to Seattle didn't really help me. I got a clean slate and then I messed it up. Wherever I go, I will be sick in the head, bipolar, treated but never to be cured. The disorder is not like kindling, I think. Fire is not a metaphor I can understand: it isn't something I can touch or experience beyond its heat. The only role fire has really had in my life was to light cigarettes—flick, burn, extinguish, and then it's gone.

Driving, though, I know. Navigating bipolar disorder seems like driving in a residential neighborhood that is not well planned out. The streets curve around like the folds of the brain. I keep going, probably blindly, choosing left or right or straight, and sometimes I'll see something beautiful—a boat, a light, a constellation—that curbs my frustration. And I can tell myself, no matter how lost I am, or how badly I have to pee, it's a nice drive, and I won't be lost for much longer. Because I have a cell phone, a firm resolve, a half tank of gas, and a GPS system. My psychiatrist gives me tools, too, hundreds of pills to swallow so that I can find my way.

Medications aim to allow the mentally ill to fit into society as much as they soothe the brain's distress. Much of my mental pain has come from a knowledge that I did not fit in because of my talking, fucking, drinking, and crying. Fitting into society is like being directed down a pink-highlighted route. When I don't fit in, I search for satellites, hoping some voice will direct me.

The car is a somewhat sterile environment. No trace of disorder, of pussy; cigarette stench obliterated by Febreeze; minimal clutter; no pill bottles or cum spots; no chance of glimpsing my round face in the mirror unless I want to; no living things but me. Always a task at hand: move. I crossed the country in a car so that I could get away from the mess I had made.

Now, the GPS lady suggests that I make a U-turn, which I must agree is the only option.

Genesis 19: The Lord brings fire and brimstone to Sodom and Gomorrah. An escaping woman looks back. The Lord turns her into a pillar of salt.

I look back and I look back and I look back. I turn into a pillar of melting guts, skin blooming with blemishes, sticky wheezing lungs, tight strap muscles, clenched vagina wounded and healing over and over. I am not the tight package I was. Fat sits over my tight muscle like scoops of ice cream. My skin is so translucent that sometimes, blue veins appear underneath it, all over my breasts and shoulders, like a lace shawl. I am still beautiful, but my outside is catching up with my insides. My brain is pickled in a bath of chemicals. My lungs bring up all the tar they can find. My skin shows barely a trace of the severe acne I had for a year.

Two years ago, in Maryland, I thought that if I weren't attractive, I would have nothing. I meant it. In my brain I believed it more than I believed anything. I had been an ugly teenager, gangly and acned, with bad glasses and crazy clothes. By the end of college, I was underweight, tanned, well-dressed. I had an expensive haircut. I didn't even need to own pimple cream. And now? In Seattle, someone of my size is not considered thin—average is overweight. Six months of acne meds and breasts that get bigger with every birth control pill switch. Second adolescence.

I try to remember that my body is not really the sum of what's visible. Nothing that's wrong with me can be solved by rubbing cream on my skin. First, I have to fix the brain—it's almost there. Second, the lungs. Third, the joints. Fourth, the fat. It will take a while, but once I fix my body, the heavens will open. I don't know why I think that. They've never been open before. But I really do believe it, a little. I used to wonder how I'd feel if I ever stopped being beautiful, and now I'm not sure whether I am beautiful anymore. I have a baby-fat face, round eyes, good shoulders, a padded torso, a swollen belly, enviably lean legs, and wavy fine-but-thick chin-length brown hair with a few grays. I troubleshoot part-by-part, but I am a unit.

Try again: I am a girl of twenty-four, five feet and six inches tall, one hundred and forty-four pounds. I have dark brown hair, big brown eyes, lean legs, weak arms, and the beginnings of an apple-type torso. That I have a lovely face is undisputed. That I might be fat is a strange obsession. I realize that I likely have very little sense of what I actually look like, and thinking back to my first diet my sophomore year of high school (six hundred calories a day), I am not sure that I ever knew. I keep trying to fix what I can't see with closed eyes.

When I was eight I learned that I had a soul. I thought it probably looked like the heart, but invisible and on fire, gray fire. The soul is supposed to unify the body, but if it doesn't exist, something else has to hold the parts together and tether them to the mind. Now I believe in nerves. They bridge the physical and the magical, running up and down the body, inside and out, but not everywhere, so when the surgeon cuts me open and sews me up, I only feel half the pain I know I should. Nerves only line five inches of the vagina. Maybe that's a shame, but for me, it's always been enough, more than enough, too much. I don't know what happens beyond where the nerves end—maybe my body hurts but keeps it secret from my brain.

It wouldn't be a surprise. My body keeps secrets all the time. I can go to the doctor, check WebMD, check my symptoms in the symptom checker, scour the forums, see who's falling apart in the exact way I'm falling apart, let the woman in the lab coat steal vials of my blood, let the other woman swab me up my nose or swab my cervix where it tickles or take a cup of my piss, but any diagnosis is just a guess. I know I wander at night, drive aimlessly, make the wrong decisions, spend too much money, and talk myself into holes, but I can't do more than let the doctor prescribe things until I calm down.

A psychiatric drug's mechanism of action is unknown. We know it makes the hurt stop. We know hurt also comes from burns and cuts, and we want to kill pain and stop blood, but it's hard to remember what pain really is: a sign that something is not right. When my throat feels torn apart, or when it hurts to walk for days, or when I've said the wrong thing to someone and I can't stop crying, I know what the pain is trying to tell me: *don't fuck up again*.

Heartache is a funny kind of pain. It is sure to get less acute, but that doesn't help. As melodramatic as I was when I was thirteen, I couldn't eat for two days after my last breakup. Will it always work like that? Make me ten years younger, leaving me as a child making snow angels in my bed, refusing the cat's attention?

Classical philosophers like Aristotle thought the heart was the place where reason and emotion originated, not the brain. Now, "heart" means something you use to feel, more like a soul, and the brain is for thinking, and they are in opposition. But the brain really does the thinking and feeling, and the heart is an organ that pumps blood all over the body, all muscle and no smarts. When I was in grade school, I was fascinated by the thought of which organ's failure would kill a person first. Artificial hearts exist, but who could ever design an artificial brain? Doctors can't even fix real ones.

When I was a little kid, my dad would catch fish in the lake and gut them in the kitchen sink. Entrails, white porcelain, dinner scraps caught in the drain. He would save the heart for me so that I could touch the swell of a spoon to the heart and watch it start to beat again. Then I would set the spoon on it and walk away while the beating faded. Some dead things are nearly alive, some live things are almost dead, and everything but babies and corpses falls in-between. Tonight I'm a little less dead than I was, because my tissues are recovering, my heart isn't working so hard, and I remember what the pain is trying to say to me: *fix it*. Constantly on a journey of self-improvement, I attempt to fix my attitude, weight, spending habits, use of time, sometimes slovenliness, treatment of others, living conditions, treatment of myself, outlook on life, nutrition, résumé, and general sweating of the small stuff. I turn to thing after thing, but it isn't until I crumble that I understand that the real thing is a sick brain: it breeds diseased actions, sick thoughts, a desperate need to just fucking fix just this one thing and then everything will be a whole lot better. It has happened before: that click into place of the one chemical piece that turns all past dread into nothing but feelings. Tonight, at my psychiatrist's suggestion, I will increase my Seroquel, and try to pray.

"Change up your shit," the GPS lady says. "I think there's, like, a turn up here.... Right. No, no, you're good, yeah, left, I know, I said 'right' but by that I meant, like, 'correct.'"

I take a weird turn and end up on some road separated from the Sound only by a row of houses. Perkins Road seems endless. It reminds me of back roads in New Jersey, but skinnier, and without signs to let me know I might run into something and die if I don't follow a curve. For two miles, my GPS attempts to find satellites. Finally, I reach a sign that tells me to turn around, because there's a dead end ahead. I turn around.

"Please drive to highlighted route," the GPS says, as though it's that easy.

"I fucking can't," I tell her. The window is open and my yell is so loud it might bring the street out of its coma. If I knew how to find the route, I wouldn't need direction, or pills, or reassurance that I am desirable. I wouldn't cry in my car in West Baltimore, looking for the road out of the decaying city, or feel that my heart was shutting down on Pennsylvania Avenue. People tell me that overcoming mental illness, or addiction, or trauma, is all about attitude. But that only goes so far. "No, I think you'll be cool," the GPS lady says. I prepare to drive around in the dark for another two hours, and to be bipolar forever, and to feel pain for the rest of my life, because feeling is better than not feeling. Acceptance is supposed to be the final stage of grief; what then?

My GPS lady says, "I've got this idea. I know you're looking to change your life. There's this thing I think you can do to fix everything that's been getting to you. It's risky, but it might be just what you've been looking for. You'll be home in no time at all."

My brain steams inside my skull, overheated as I consider driving my car into the Sound, surfacing, and binding my busted legs into a mermaid's tail. I never change—not a lot, anyway, and not for the better—but that's because every series of small improvements falls like a row of books on a long library shelf, dust clouds paired with tiny thuds. I don't want small changes: I want to turn half-creature and breathe through gills, replace my human brain with something that needs to only know smell and light and balance, an understanding of pain without nuance and shade.

I tell my GPS, "Fucking tell me where to go and I will."

Ten seconds later, she tells me.

END

Biographical Note

Elissa Washuta, a member of the Cowlitz Indian Tribe, was born in New Jersey and now lives in Seattle. She received an MFA in creative writing from the University of Washington in 2009 and has been the recipient of an Artist Trust GAP Award, a Potlatch Fund Native Arts Grant, a 4Culture Grant, and a Made at Hugo House Fellowship. Her work has appeared in *Salon*, *The Chronicle of Higher Education* and *Third Coast*. She is an adviser and lecturer in American Indian Studies at the University of Washington. *My Body Is a Book of Rules* is her first book.

CPSIA information can be obtained
at www.ICGtesting.com
Printed in the USA
BVHW010947230919
559149BV00001B/1/P

9 781597 099691